The Forty-ninth and

Other Parallels

The Forty-ninth and Other Parallels

Contemporary

Canadian

Perspectives

Edited with an introduction by

David Staines

The University of Massachusetts Press

Amherst   1986

87- 135

Copyright © 1986 by The University of Massachusetts Press
All rights reserved
Printed in the United States of America
Set in Linotron Galliard at G & S Typesetters, Inc.

Library of Congress Cataloging-in-Publication Data

The Forty-ninth and other parallels.

1. Canada—Civilization—1945–   .   2. Canada—
Politics and government—1980–   .   3. Canada—
Economic conditions—1945–   . I. Staines, David,
1946–   .
FI021.2.F67   1986   971.064   86–6950
ISBN 0–87023–528–1 (alk. paper)
ISBN 0–87023–529–X (pbk.: alk. paper)

The essays in this volume originated in public lectures under the auspices of the
Five-College Program in Canadian Studies, and the Program acknowledges the
generous support of the Exxon Education Foundation.

By an odd chance the forty-ninth parallel,
an astronomical line,
turned out to *mean* something.

STEPHEN LEACOCK

Contents

The Forty-ninth and

Other Parallels

David Staines

Introduction

The world's longest undefended border—five thousand miles of it—separates Canada from the United States and acknowledges two distinct nations that divide between themselves virtually an entire continent.

Proximity to the United States has been a constant factor in Canada's political, economic, and cultural development. To the Canadian, the United States has a powerful continental presence, friendly and supportive, but also threatening and ominous.

In his 1960 collection of essays, *A Voice from the Attic,* Robertson Davies described his country as an attic. Two decades later, Mordecai Richler moved on from this image: "This country, 116 years old but still blurry, is like a child's kaleidoscope that remains in urgent need of one more sharp twist of the barrel to bring everything into sharp focus. Making us whole. Something more than this continent's attic."

According to Margaret Atwood, Canada stands in marked contrast to the United States:

Canada sees itself as part of the world; a small sinking Titanic squashed between two icebergs, perhaps, but still inevitably a part. The States, on the other hand, has always had a little trouble with games like chess. Situational strategy is difficult if all you can see is your own borders, and beyond that some wispy brownish fuzz that is barely worth considering. The Canadian experience was a circumference with no centre, the American one a centre which was mistaken for the whole thing.

When Marshall McLuhan contemplated the Canadian experience, he reflected on Canada's ability to define itself in the light of its southern neighbor:

> Canada has become the anti-environment that renders the United States more acceptable and intelligible to many small countries of the world; anti-environments are indispensable for making an environment understandable. Canada has no goals or directions, yet shares so much of the American character and experience that the role of dialogue and liaison has become entirely natural to Canadians wherever they are.

At the same time, he noted, Canada can help the United States define itself: "Sharing the American way, without commitment to American goals or responsibilities, makes the Canadian intellectually detached and observant as an interpreter of the American destiny." Canada can and does provide a unique perspective on the United States.

In 1982 I accepted an invitation to be Five College Professor of Canadian Studies. The Five Colleges, a consortium consisting of Amherst College, Hampshire College, Mount Holyoke College, Smith College, and the University of Massachusetts at Amherst, initiated formal cooperation in Canadian Studies in 1977 with the appointment of John J. Conway as Professor of Canadian Studies and director of the Five College Program in Canadian Studies. The location was appropriate: Smith College became the first American college or university to teach Quebec literature when Marine Leland introduced such a course in 1940. Even before then, offerings in Canadian history and Canadian government appeared in Smith's curriculum. The program was designed to give faculty and students a continental perspective on problems common to Canada and the United States within the context of their different cultures.

I had the opportunity to introduce courses on Canadian literature in the departments of English at Mount Holyoke College, Smith College, and the University of Massachusetts at Amherst. In addition, through the financial assistance of the Canadian Consulate General in Boston, I was able to invite distinguished public figures from Canada to visit the consortium and address faculty and students, both in formal lectures and in informal seminars, on their professions or professional commitments. The Canadian-American border keeps Canadians, Marshall McLuhan concluded, "in a perpetual philosophic mood which nourishes flexibility in the absence of strong commitments or definite goals. By contrast, the United States, with heavy commitments and sharply defined objectives, is not in a good position to be philosophic, or cool, or flexible."

The guests were asked not only to explore their world from a Canadian perspective, but also to relate that world, implicitly or explicitly, to the United States. The insights of these Canadian observers shaped this volume. Developing and expanding the ideas they expressed at the Five Colleges, the authors have prepared this series of original commentaries on important dimensions of the Canadian scene and, by comparison and contrast, the American scene.

It is significant that the observers are informed authorities on contemporary Canada who do not hesitate to regard Canada in its continental context. Viewing their own country in this fashion, they write with clarity and honesty of Canada's achievements and shortcomings, often emphasizing the significance of two independent countries on one continent.

The Forty-ninth and Other Parallels begins with three essays on the implications of a nation of two founding peoples, English and French. In "Canada: The Challenge of Coexistence," Victor C. Goldbloom, president of the Canadian Council of Christians and Jews, presents a commentary on the frequent comparison of Canada as a social mosaic and the United States as a melting pot. From his legal and judicial perspective, Thomas R. Berger, professor of law and former provincial Supreme Court judge, makes the new Canadian Constitution and the Charter of Rights and Freedoms (1982) the focus for his reflections on the diversity of the Canadian experience. The question of French-language rights concerns Gérald Godin, former Quebec Minister of Cultural Communities and Immigration, who, speaking from the perspective of the Parti Québécois, assesses the significance of the Charter of the French Language, Quebec's Bill 101 (1977).

The new Constitution and the Charter of Rights and Freedoms guaranteed equality for women, and Judy Erola, former Minister Responsible for the Status of Women, played a major role in the creation of this historic legislation. In "Women in the Eighties," she offers her personal account of the uniquely Canadian forces that led to the Constitution's including rights for women.

Canada's economic dependence upon the United States, long a vexatious issue, has prompted many to regard Canada as a colony that has paid allegiance to three mother countries: France, then England, and now the United States. Economist and educator H. Ian Macdonald studies the obstacles to technological innovation existing in Canada in the eighties.

Both Canada and the United States are democracies, the Canadian parliamentary, the American republican, and each is characterized by two mainstream political parties, the Liberals and the Progressive Conservatives in Canada and the Democrats and the Republicans in the United States. A major distinction is the continuing presence in Canada of a social democratic third party, the New Democrats, on both the federal and the provincial levels. Bob Rae, leader of the Ontario New Democratic Party, analyses the three-party system, wondering why the United States, alone among Western industrial democracies, has no social democratic party.

Monique Bégin, former Minister of National Health and Welfare, assumed major responsibility for the passage of the Canada Health Act (1984). In "Medicare—Available to All Canadians," she writes about the history of the act, wondering why Americans will not easily, if ever, see a universal, free health system adopted in their country.

The written word is the focus of the two closing essays. From his long career in journalism on both sides of the border, Walter Stewart defines "The Seven Myths of Journalism," reflecting on their applicability in Canada and the United States. In his career in education, novelist and poet Robert Kroetsch has been both student and teacher in the two countries. In "Canadian Writing: No Name Is My Name," he explores Canadian literature, a twentieth-century creation, finding patterns that distinguish it from American literature, which reached maturity in the nineteenth century.

The Forty-ninth and Other Parallels is a testimony to two destinies that have shaped and are shaping North America. The individual essays, focusing on contemporary Canada, never lose sight of continental realities beyond the merely geographical, thereby commenting on two countries that seem to have developed in parallel. "The word 'parallel' is important," Northrop Frye observed. "Canada may be an American colony, as is often said, by me among others, but Canadians have never thought of the United States as a parental figure, like Britain, and analogies of youthful revolt and the like would be absurd."

For more than a century, the Canadian-American border has stood undefended. But history reveals that the border, seldom free of offensives, was created and defined by centuries of disputes and skirmishes, treaties and legislation. The seemingly illogical border in the eastern part of the continent, for example, still reflects economic and political interests of the fur trade in the sixteenth and seventeenth centuries. And the forty-ninth parallel, established in 1818 as the border from northwestern Ontario to the Rockies and extended in 1846 to the Pacific Coast, is, George Woodcock noted, "a compromise boundary reached in negotiations dominated by acquisitiveness in Washington and a desire in Westminster for North American peace at almost any price. The Canadians have always felt betrayed by the various territorial agreements reached during the nineteenth century between Britain and the United States, and on grounds of history and geography alike they were justified." Like many parallels, the forty-ninth, unguarded now, is superficially deceptive.

The Forty-ninth and Other Parallels addresses contemporary issues from a Canadian perspective. Canada's similarities to the United States obscure profound differences in ideas, in political and social attitudes, and in values. Superficial parallels exist, but they reveal, on close examination, major distinctions and differences. Unable to ignore the border separating Canada from the United States, the nine essayists examine continental realities as they explore some unique features, historical and political, economic and cultural, of the nation north of the forty-ninth parallel.

Victor C. Goldbloom

Canada: The Challenge of Coexistence

The very existence of Canada is, and has always been, a challenge. Almost a century younger than the United States, larger in geographic area but with only one-tenth the population, limited by its northerly, intemperate climate to shorter growing seasons and condemned to costly lighting and heating during its longer winters of briefer daylight, Canada has faced the additional challenge of carving out a distinctive identity and playing a constructive role on the international stage.

When the forty-ninth parallel was established as a major portion of the boundary between Canada and the United States, the viability of the northern entity was very much in doubt. Throughout Canada's formative years, considerable opinion held that amalgamation with the United States was inevitable; many of that opinion felt such amalgamation desirable and even fought politically for its achievement. Even among those who actively resisted that thought, probably the majority, there was appreciable apprehension and unease. Eventually, slowly, the necessary leadership emerged.

Sir John A. Macdonald, Canada's first prime minister (1867–74 and again 1878–91), provided the vision and the driving force. He applied the latter, however, in much the same way that Quintus Fabius Maximus contrived the defeat of Hannibal, and like that Roman general, who acquired the sobriquet of *cunctator* (the delayer), he became known as "Old Tomorrow." As the record testifies, he succeeded against what sometimes seemed insurmountable odds. For Canadians, who tend to be somewhat undernourished in their own history, Donald Creighton's biography of him is a revelation as suspenseful as a John le Carré novel and as engaging as a Thomas Hardy tale. He was the almost single-handed architect of the country we know today.

His vision required that the country be bound together, from sea to sea, and his thread was the railroad. Stubbornly he pushed it westward, through swamp and barren rockland, from financial crisis to financial crisis, disregarding the easier route through the United States territory south of the Great Lakes and up into western Canada through Minnesota, North Dakota, or even Montana. The steel rails forged the nation and became the lifeline of its viability and its subsequent growth. Sir John A., with a different kind of victory, became as much the father of his country as George Washington had been of his.

Canada today has ten provinces and two territories; the United States today has fifty states and a number of other territorial components. Each country began as a fragment of the entity we now know. Just as the United States was formed out of thirteen original colonies, so Canada at Confederation in 1867 had only four original provinces: Nova Scotia, New Brunswick, Quebec, and Ontario. The others either evolved as wide open spaces were settled, cleared, and planted, or joined by voluntary amalgamation, as did Newfoundland in 1949. The challenge of coexistence became the reality of each and every day.

Let me take two steps back and refer to two problems of coexistence that antedated the political union of the country. Both are still with Canadians; indeed, both are very much part of today's reality. One is held in common with the United States; the other is distinctly Canadian, and in fact constitutes a major component of that which distinguishes Canada from its distinguished neighbor to the south.

When Jacques Cartier sailed up the St. Lawrence River in 1534, the problem of coexistence between native and nonnative peoples began. Of all the challenges I shall discuss, this is the one Canadians have met the least successfully, the one in which they can take the least pride. Nonnative settlers displaced the native peoples, competed with them economically, fought with them, involved them on both sides of French-English wars, and ultimately humiliated them, dispossessed them, and confined them to tiny territorial enclaves. Only in fairly recent years, as with the conclusion of an important agreement between the government of Quebec and the Indian and Inuit peoples of the James Bay territory with respect to the massive hydroelectric project now being implemented in that area, has there begun to appear a significant commitment to redressment and mutual respect. Paternalism is diminishing slowly; concomitantly, the involvement of native peoples in the larger society around them is starting, little by little, to grow. Reciprocal trust, for so long a scarce commodity, is beginning to reappear.

The challenge of coexistence between native and nonnative peoples has taken on a new immediacy with the substantial migration, especially in western Canada, of native Indians from the reserves to the cities. In Calgary and Edmonton, in Saskatoon, Regina, and Winnipeg, civic authorities and community organizations have set about providing information and smoothing adjustments. In a larger metropolitan area like Toronto, however, the presence of some ten thousand native Indians is much less obvious and has not been the object of so focused a response. In a number of cities, the Canadian Council of Christians and Jews has undertaken two kinds of educational programs: integrative training for native peoples with regard to urban society, to public authority, to health and social services, to the educational system, and to the economy in general, as well as the provision of meeting places for their own purpose; and sensitivity or "native awareness" courses, alone or within a broader context of intercultural education, for teachers, social workers, police officers, nurses, civil servants, and community leaders. Support and guidance for native industries and businesses are also being developed by people of goodwill.

The second challenge of coexistence, one that continues to pervade Canadian political life, arose in 1759 when the British defeated the French at Quebec City in the Battle of the Plains of Abraham. Canada has been a part of the British Empire or Commonwealth ever since, yet six million of its twenty-five million people are French-speaking Canadians, and their unshakable commitment to their language, culture, and view of Canadian history constitutes a force with which no government can fail to reckon.

The concentration of French-speaking Canadians in the province of Quebec, more than five million out of the six million, causes the history of that province, and of the province's relations with the rest of Canada, to be a focal element in the analysis of this complex challenge. Language has become the most sensitive component of the average Canadian's sense of identity, the one that emits the strongest (and often the most unreasoning) emotion when touched; religion, which used to have that characteristic, has faded in reactivity in recent years. Survival, the assurance of a continuity from a living past to a living posterity, is seen in linguistic terms by Canadians wherever their language group is locally, regionally, or nationally in the minority.

When the British took over, they set out to assuage the bitterness of defeat by abstaining from suppressing the French language. Today, with pointed irony, many French-speaking Canadians, including militant nationalists, will observe that if the British had taken advantage of the aftermath of their conquest to make Canada a unilingual English-speaking country, Canada would not be struggling with linguistic coexistence. Success has been only partial and relative, but there is more goodwill (and more effective bilingualism) in evidence today than at any time in memory. It would be virtually unthinkable for a national political party to choose a leader today who was unable to function reasonably in both Canadian languages.

At various times in Canadian history, political leaders have worked in tandem to bridge the gap between French and English: Louis-Hippolyte Lafontaine and Robert Baldwin, joint premiers of United Canada in the 1840s, Sir John A. Macdonald and Sir George-Etienne Cartier, joint premiers of United Canada in the era of Confederation, and many more. Notwithstanding their efforts and indeed their achievements, however, Quebec has always felt different from the rest of Canada and has always sought the recognition of a particular status within Confederation—and, failing that recognition, has, with various degrees of intensity, at various times given serious consideration to secession.

Until 1960, a watershed date in the history of Quebec, the social and economic characteristics of French-Canadian society were such that in a certain sense, especially for the mass of the population, life was lived somewhat separately from the rest of Canada. Maurice Duplessis, premier of the province for much of the 1940s and 1950s, frequently inveighed against "those who would deprive us of" a variety of values, traditions, and decisional autonomies; but behind the rhetoric was a tacit and comfortable modus vivendi with the federal authority in Ottawa, and there was no significant separatist movement in the province's political spectrum. Then, in 1960, Quebec made its belated, dramatic, whirlwind entry into the twentieth century.

That entry came to be called the Quiet Revolution, and its architect was the new premier, Jean Lesage. Previously a minister in the federal government of Lester B. Pearson, and throughout his life an unequivocal federalist, he threw open the doors and minds of Quebec society, letting great gusts of fresh air into education, into health care and social services, into economic activity, and into the province's external relations. New challenges of coexistence became part of Canadian life.

It was historically inevitable that the winds of change should stir Quebec nationalism. The heady discovery of abilities to do things that had never been done before, to compete in areas that had previously been left to others, to emerge from inhibitions imposed by a more conservative view of society and life, was essentially irresistible. Suddenly, Quebec felt it could do anything; on the fringes of the major, fundamental, central achievements through which Lesage led the province, people were impatient to ride off, like Stephen Leacock's horseman, madly in all directions.

Six years later, Quebec was too breathless to sustain the pace, and Lesage met unpredicted defeat. Expectations having outstripped fulfillments, frustrations had begun to burst out; Ottawa, English Canada, and the federal system were obvious targets, and they were taxed (not without justification) with slowness and in-adequacy in their responses to Quebec's new aspirations. Less than a year and a half after the defeat of the Lesage government, René Lévesque, who had been one of the most conspicuous ministers in that government, walked out of the Quebec Liberal party and founded the separatist movement.

Coexistence, said the separatists, was impossible. Only an autonomous, self-governing entity could ensure linguistic and cultural survival. The French-speaking Canadian, immediately upon crossing the borders of Quebec, was (except for small areas of eastern Ontario and northern New Brunswick) in hostile territory where virtually no one cared for the French language, showed courtesy to anyone speaking it, or gave more than lip service to the bilingual nature of Canada. The federal government was prejudiced against Quebec, any French-speaking members of the federal Parliament were *vendus* (sellouts), and Quebec taxpayers poured far more into federal coffers than they received back in federal contributions and investments. In addition, among the scores of new countries coming to independence and taking their places in the councils of the United Nations, few had larger populations than Quebec and none had comparable resources and skills.

Although these and companion arguments have never succeeded in convincing a majority of Quebecers, time and the complexities of the democratic process eventually, in 1976, brought the Parti Québécois to power. As legislative and administrative measures fostered French and diminished English, some English-speaking Canadians left the province; most remained, however, and there arose from among them a coordinated movement, which took the name Alliance Quebec, dedicated to the defense of English-language institutions in the province and also to the pursuit of constructive coexistence.

In the spring of 1980, the Parti Québécois held its promised referendum on separation. Despite a question formulated to avoid directly posing the issue of separation, 59.5 percent voted to remain in Canada, with the separatist cause gaining a majority in only 17 percent of Quebec's 110 electoral districts. Most analysts, including me, concluded that a battle had been won but that the war would go on; in fact, it soon became evident that the majority felt that the referendum result had been a definitive, virtually permanent decision, binding for at least a generation—so less than a year later, they reelected the Parti Québécois.

The debate goes on, to be sure. Underlying it is a fundamental issue which is not only political but philosophical as well, and which has, on each side, historical roots in the respective traditions of French-speaking and English-speaking people: collective rights and concerns versus individual rights and freedoms. French-speaking Canadians—in large majority, not only those whose option is separatism—feel a collective responsibility for the survival of the French language and culture in the North American context, overwhelmingly English, and feel that their defensive position (being scarcely more than 2 percent of the continent's total population) requires, not only of the English-speaking minority in the province but of themselves as well, some sacrifice of individual freedoms of choice. One of the difficulties inherent in communication, and therefore in coexistence, between French-speaking and English-speaking Canadians is that vocabulary and phraseology, philosophy and dialectic, are not identical. Much progress, however, is being made in this regard, and in simple linguistic ability as well. The outlook for meaningful, mutually respectful, truly friendly coexistence is better today than at any time since 1759.

Some twenty years ago, listening to a French-language radio station in my car on my way to make a pediatric house call, I heard a rather poetic evocation of an imaginary conversation between two trees. One said to the other (I paraphrase), "We've stood here in the forest, near each other, for such a long time, and we've never spoken. I'm sure we have much in common, much that we could share in terms of thoughts, experiences, and concerns, much that we could enjoy together as the years go by." And so on for several minutes. Finally, the other tree replied, and said, "Sorry, I don't speak French." That was the Canada of yesterday; it will not be the Canada of tomorrow.

Let me return now to Sir John A. Macdonald, the railroad, and the unification of the country. As settlement moved westward, largely adjacent to the right-of-way, the composition of Canada's population changed. The east, after the fall of the French regime, had been peopled primarily by emigrants from the British Isles, with Scots especially conspicuous among them; the west drew settlers from central and eastern Europe as well, and the Pacific Coast began to attract people from the Orient. Each region came, therefore, to have its own historical attachments and cultural traditions; each came to perceive the history and evolution of Canada in terms of the history and contributions of its principal ethnic groups.

The railroad, Sir John A.'s thread for sewing the country together, brought with it a certain number of promises and enticements. Significant among these was the sense of belonging to a new, untapped, exciting country, a land of opportunity, which, unlike the United States, had not rejected its relations with Britain. Bread and butter were also, as always, important, and so the reduction of transportation costs for necessities moving westward and products moving eastward weighed heavily in the west's decision to join. Here, too, expectations outstripped fulfillments, and in time gave way to disappointment and even to disillusion. Regionalism became a feature of Canadian life.

Distance, then, is also a part of the challenge of coexistence. The west has for some time felt alienated from the rest of Canada, discriminated against by transportation costs, and coerced into accepting a two-language, two-founding-peoples Canada when it perceives only a comparatively small multicultural society with a limited French-speaking population. Healing leadership has been lacking, but it will come; when it does, the truth and validity of Sir John A.'s vision will shine again as they did in 1867.

About a decade ago, Canada made a profound political and sociological decision: it defined itself as a multicultural country. Initially, the concept was simplistic: immigrants from different parts of the world should be helped to preserve their cultural and artistic traditions as enriching contributions to the Canadian whole. Rather quickly, Canadian understanding and perceptivity evolved: multiculturalism became intercultural education, the response to the challenge of multicultural coexistence within a single country.

This definition of Canada often gives rise to an oversimplified comparison: the United States is a melting pot, Canada is a multicultural mosaic. The comparison contains some measure of truth, to be sure, but it does not stand up under thoughtful analysis.

For all its affirmation of its multicultural composition, Canada cannot help being a melting pot as well. Except for its native peoples, the country has grown by immigration, and each post-immigration generation has inevitably relinquished some of its original distinctiveness and merged into a certain uniform identity. At the same time, one of Canada's major continuing challenges is to convince itself, and large numbers of its citizens, that the notion of multiculturalism, the notion of two languages and two founding peoples, and the notion of a unique Canadian identity are not incompatible with each other.

It would not be appropriate for me to comment critically upon the United States. Let me nevertheless be bold enough to share an observation made by an American, the Reverend John T. Walker, Episcopal bishop of Washington, D. C. A few years ago Bishop Walker was in Kamloops, British Columbia, at the invitation of the Anglican bishop of that diocese, to address a gathering of the Canadian Council of Christians and Jews. He spoke of the sociological differences between Canada and the United States; he spoke in particular of the American dream and the American melting pot. The American dream, he said, the dream of opportunity and the dream that any citizen, of no matter what origin or humble beginnings, might one day become president, undoubtedly has a significant measure of validity. Remember, however, he went on, that the American melting pot has never melted down the black, the Asiatic, the Native American. . . . Coexistence, according to his conclusion (these words are my paraphrase, unlike those which precede), is a complex challenge in human sensitivity.

There is a considerable problem inherent in a multicultural society: majority rule becomes too simplistic to be a valid expression of democracy. Where the particular interests of minorities are at stake, government must make itself the conscience of the majority and act legislatively to protect those interests if they risk being ignored or overridden by simple majority vote. It is often said, with justification, that the quality and effectiveness of democratic systems must be judged by their protection of their minorities.

Finally, let me examine Canada's management of a universal

problem of coexistence, the unequal distribution of wealth and resources among the country's population. Few societies today, of course, can credibly claim to be purely capitalist or purely socialist. Canada's economy is closest to the American model and has a high degree of interdependence with it; yet in health care, social services, pension plans, legal aid, and education, Canada has instituted publicly funded systems which have essentially eliminated financial barriers to universal, equal access. Tax levels tend, therefore, to be somewhat higher than in the United States, but they remain a good deal lower than those in Britain or the Scandinavian countries.

The professionals who provide these various services have, by and large, come to terms with the payment systems. They are widely unionized and negotiate accordingly, a condition quite unfamiliar to their American counterparts in many service fields. All is not always smooth, and there have even been strikes of physicians, nurses, and other hospital personnel; yet if providers and recipients were offered the opportunity to turn the clock back, it is clear that an overwhelming majority would refuse.

There are still rich and poor in Canada; there are still inequalities and even injustices, and the public conscience continues to struggle with them. Canada is not a socialist society; reward for initiative, imagination, and effort remains a very real incentive. Canada has, however, done much to relieve financial anxiety in the lower economic levels of the population in the face of fundamental needs.

Coexistence is a challenge; it is also an opportunity, and indeed a responsibility. In a world overfilled with hostility and hatred, tribalism and mistrust, Canadians hope, modestly but with cautious confidence, that they can be a model of harmony and mutual respect.

Thomas R. Berger

Human Rights in Canada: The English, the French, and the Native Peoples

On April 17, 1982, Canada adopted a new Constitution and, at the same time, a Charter of Rights and Freedoms. Together they represent, I believe, a valuable and uniquely Canadian undertaking.

The new Constitution and Charter of Rights (the Charter, like the United States Bill of Rights, is part of the Constitution itself) are the outcome of a debate that lasted a year and more. In fact, the debate had lasted for more than a century. In 1867, when the British Parliament enacted Canada's original constitution, the British North America Act, Canada's founding fathers neglected to include a provision for amending it and their successors were never able to agree on an amending procedure. This means that every amendment since 1867 has had to be passed by the British Parliament. Pierre Trudeau, therefore, developed his proposal for an amending formula and a Charter of Rights and Freedoms:

Canada would go back to the British Parliament and ask it to include in the original constitution both a means by which Canadians could amend it and a Charter of Rights and Freedoms. This would leave Canada with a fully fledged constitution that included a charter.

In the debate over "bringing home the Constitution" at last, we were called upon to articulate our idea of Canada. Why do we believe in Canada? What things are most important in our shared history? Why is Canada worth preserving in the 1980s?

Canada, twenty-five million souls scattered amongst the snow and scenery, has persisted. Why? And why should it matter? Canadians are well acquainted with the main themes of their history: New France, the fur trade, the establishment of British institutions. Historians used to maintain that Canada's story was essentially one of transition from colony to nation, of the achievement of self-government within the British Empire, in defiance of geography. But then Harold Innis stood this idea on its head: he said that it was, in fact, Canadian geography that had made possible our existence as a nation. He denied that the Canadian economy was simply a series of northward projections from the economic heartland of North America. Others have suggested that it is a northern tradition that makes Canada distinct from the United States today. We share a mass culture with the United States, but it is Canada that has, and always has had, a distinct northern geography and a special concern with the North.

None of these theories, however, constitutes an intellectual tradition. None of these tells us what is the cement in the Canadian constitutional edifice. What binds us together today, and will bind us together tomorrow?

Some believe that the Canadian achievement lies in the utilization of natural resources—the establishment of the fishery, the gathering of fur, the development of the grain trade, the building of an empire in timber, and more recently the exploitation of oil and gas and minerals on our frontiers and beyond. Here lies the Canadian achievement, in the conquest of cold and distant landscapes and seascapes. These common enterprises, it is said, are what unite us all.

But is there not more to it than that? Is there not a Canadian intellectual contribution to the legal and political order—a product of the encounter of the English and the French in North America—which is distinctive because it represents something essentially Canadian?

Western nations cherish representative institutions and the rule of law, democracy, and due process. Their traditions affirm the right to dissent: in politics, in religion, in science, and in the arts. And all these traditions, it seems to me, will be strengthened by the Constitution and Charter of Rights. We conceive of our rights as individual rights, but they are more than that. They are the means whereby diversity is maintained, and whereby minorities can thrive.

Much has been said about the Americanization of the Canadian Constitution, by the adoption of a Charter of Rights. Our new Constitution and Charter of Rights, however, take us beyond the American Constitution and Bill of Rights.

The American Constitution and Bill of Rights were adopted in the late eighteenth century. The Bill of Rights is a classic statement of liberal ideas of *individual* rights, of the political and legal rights that appertain to individual liberty. In Canada these have been safeguarded by the common law, and have by and large been observed as faithfully as in the United States. Now they have been included (though not altogether entrenched) in the Canadian Constitution and Charter of Rights. It is to a consideration of these provisions of the Constitution and Charter that lawyers are usually drawn. (In 1960, Parliament passed a Bill of Rights, but it had no more force than any federal law, and the courts were reluctant to apply it; in any event, its provisions were not as wide ranging as those of the Charter of Rights.)

The Canadian Constitution and Charter of Rights, however, go further than the American Constitution and Bill of Rights. Reflecting twentieth-century notions of freedom, they include explicit protection for the rights of minorities. The rights of both of Canada's great linguistic communities have been recognized in the Constitution and the Charter. The special place of the native people—the Indians, the Inuit, and the Metis—has been acknowledged. The Charter of Rights has acknowledged the multi-cultural dimension of Canadian society by guaranteeing to every individual the right to equality under the law and the right to the equal protection of the law "without discrimination based on race, national or ethnic origin, [or] colour."

In Canada we have two great societies, two nations, if you will. It would be a mistake to pretend otherwise. We are mixed up together, and we have chosen to stay together. There are a million or more native people in our midst, claiming a measure of self-determination, and there are millions of new Canadians—immigrants of every ethnic and racial background and every political and religious persuasion. Thus diversity is the essence of the Canadian experience. The Constitution and the Charter reflect this diversity.

Does this leave us with a constitutional hodge-podge: protection for languages here, over there guarantees for aboriginal peoples, and, as well, an affirmation of multiculturalism? No, these measures are the logical outcome of our history. If Quebec were to achieve independence, it would at once be faced with the very questions that confront Canadians: the rights of a great linguistic minority, the claims of the aboriginal peoples, and the place of numerous ethnic and racial groups in the life of the country.

Our concepts of self-government acquired their present form in the nation-states of Great Britain and France, states that have traditionally been ethnically defined; we have not, therefore, fully realized or developed institutional guarantees for racial, cultural, religious, and linguistic minorities. In the British North America Act of 1867, we made a beginning: in the new Constitution and the Charter, we have made an advance.

Our Constitution has always recognized that we are a plural, not a monolithic society. This is what is best in the Canadian tradition. It has meant that refugees from every continent, immigrants of every race, peoples of all faiths and those seeking political asylum—all have found their place in Canadian life. On a per capita basis, Canada accepted a larger number of "boat people" than any other country. In fact, Canada now has the world's highest ratio of refugees to total population—one in every 324 Canadians is a refugee.

It is our good fortune that we are not all of common descent, that we do not speak one language only. We are not cursed with a triumphant ideology; we are not given to mindless patriotism.

For these reasons Canada is a difficult country to govern. There is no easy consensus. It would be simpler if we all spoke the same language, if all our children went to the same schools, if we all held the same religious beliefs, if we were all one color. But we are not. Such diversity should not terrify us, or provoke an epidemic of xenophobia. It is our strength, not our weakness.

The struggles of Canada's minorities do not represent all of the Canadian experience, but they throw into relief the true extent of our capacity for tolerance, our belief in diversity. They sharpen our perception of ourselves—and though many of these struggles began long ago, they still continue—and they will have a contemporary denouement. Along every seam in the Canadian mosaic unraveled by conflict, a thread of tolerance can still be seen. I speak of tolerance as a positive quality, not as mere indifference, of tolerance as the expression of a profound conviction about the virtues of diversity and the rights of minorities.

The crises of times past have thrown up men and women who have articulated an idea of Canada that illuminates the Canadian journey, and I wish to cite the words of three of them: Wilfrid Laurier, Angus MacInnis, and Emmett Hall.

Wilfrid Laurier's career spanned the three school crises of the French-Canadian minorities in Canada. He was a Liberal backbencher in the House of Commons in the 1870s when the Acadians in New Brunswick lost their claim to constitutional guarantees for their denominational schools. As Canada's first French-Canadian prime minister, he negotiated the Laurier-Greenway agreement in 1896, which gave to French Canadians in Manitoba the right to conduct religious teaching in the public schools after hours. He was in opposition again when the Ontario government sought to limit the use of French in the separate schools of Ontario in 1912.

The disputes about separate schools in New Brunswick in the 1870s, in Manitoba in the 1890s, and in Ontario in the early years of this century were not simply disputes about religion and schools, curriculum and language. They were disputes about the place of French Canadians in English-speaking provinces. In New Brunswick and in Manitoba the dispute was ostensibly over religion, in Ontario over language—two different carriers of culture. But in each case the underlying issue was the same: were French Canadians to have a distinct and inviolate place in the life of English-speaking provinces, to be free to practice their religion and speak their language, not as a private matter, but as a matter of constitutional right, and to have the same entitlement to public funds for their denominational schools as the provinces provided to the English-language public schools?

Laurier, no longer prime minister, was leader of the Opposition when Ontario sought to limit the use of French in the bilingual schools of that province. On May 9, 1916, the Liberals moved a resolution in the House of Commons urging the Legislative Assembly of Ontario not to interfere with the children of French-speaking parents being taught in their mother tongue. Laurier spoke in support of that resolution. He expressed his belief that every child in Ontario ought to be able to speak English, but he pleaded for the right of the children of French parentage to a second education in a second language. Here is Laurier, in his seventies, still able to summon eloquence and passion:

> Now I come to the point where I want to speak to my fellow-countrymen in the province of Ontario. When I ask that every child of my own race should receive an English education, will you refuse us the privilege of education also in the language of our mothers and fathers? That is all that I ask today; I ask nothing more than that. I simply ask you, my fellow-countrymen, British subjects like myself, if, when we say that we must have an English education, you will say: "You shall have an English education and nothing else." There are men who say that in the schools of Ontario and Manitoba there should be no other language than the English language. But, sir, when I ask that we should have also the benefit of a French education, will you refuse that benefit? Is that an unnatural demand? Is that an obnoxious demand? Will the con-

cession of it do harm to anybody? And will it be said that in the great province of Ontario there is a disposition to put a bar on knowledge and to stretch every child in the schools of Ontario upon a Procrustean bed and say that they shall all be measured alike, that no one shall have the privilege of a second education in a single language?

In the end, Laurier failed. The French-Canadian minorities have survived, but without constitutional guarantees. Laurier could only plead for what he called "the regime of tolerance." He could not claim it for French Canadians as a constitutional right. In the new Charter of Rights, however, there is a constitutional guarantee for minority language-education rights. This provision can be the means by which the French language is maintained in English-speaking provinces.

But, some will say, why should there be language guarantees for French Canadians? Why should their schools be protected under the Charter of Rights? One might equally well ask, why should there be language guarantees for the English-speaking minority in Quebec? Why should their schools be protected? The French were the first Europeans to settle in the Maritimes and on the St. Lawrence, and the first to explore the west. They did not arrive in Canada expecting to assimilate. They were there all along. They are one of the two founding peoples of Canada, and entitled to retain their own language and their own culture anywhere in Canada.

This is important not only to French Canadians. The preservation of French-language rights in the English-speaking provinces is, in the long run, likely to preserve English-language rights in Quebec. Moreover, though the French and English languages are constitutionally protected, and thus stand on a different footing from the languages of other ethnic groups in Canada, they are in a sense a bulwark for those languages. By negating the idea of a monolithic culture, constitutional protection of French and English makes the way easier for other languages. Thus official bilingualism and biculturalism is not a rejection but an affirmation of multiculturalism, of the idea of Canada as a mosaic, a country where diversity is cherished. This was Laurier's vision of Canada. Rejecting the American ideal of the melting pot, he thought of Canada as a Gothic cathedral:

> a harmonious whole, in which granite, marble, oak and other materials are blended. This cathedral is the image of the nation that I hope to see Canada become. As long as I live, as long as I have the power to labour in the service of my country, I shall repel the idea of changing the nature of its different elements. I want the marble to remain the marble; I want the granite to remain the granite; I want the oak to remain the oak.

Nineteen eighty-two was the fortieth anniversary of the expulsion of the Japanese Canadians from the Pacific Coast. In Canada, this anniversary led to reflection on the causes of that unhappy event. The expulsion of the Japanese Canadians in 1942 was not the result of a sudden manifestation of anti-Japanese feeling in British Columbia. The province had a long history of animosity toward Orientals and a long history of discriminatory legislation. Racism had been entrenched in the province's political culture and enshrined in federal and provincial statutes. Waves of anti-Oriental feeling had many times lapped at the homes of the Japanese Canadians. In June 1941, there were 22,096 persons of Japanese descent in British Columbia, 76.39 percent of them Canadian born, but Pearl Harbor generated a wave of anti-Japanese hysteria which was to sweep the Japanese Canadians away, to disperse them and to destroy their communities.

Japanese Canadians were anxious and apprehensive as war with Japan drew ever closer. Throughout 1941, members of Parliament from British Columbia urged the federal government to take drastic measures against the Japanese Canadians. Only one member from the province, Angus MacInnis of the Co-operative Commonwealth Federation (Canada's social democratic party, now the New Democratic Party), defended the Japanese Canadians. Here is MacInnis speaking in the House of Commons on February 25, 1941:

> If we are to have harmonious and friendly relations between the

oriental population and the rest of our British Columbia citizens, we must stop discriminating against and abusing the orientals. We must find some common ground on which we can work, and I think it can be found. Is there any reason, if we should get into difficulties with Japan on the Pacific coast, why the Japanese in British Columbia should be interested in helping Canada, after the way in which we are treating them? I am satisfied that if we treat the Japanese and our other oriental citizens aright, we shall get their loyalty, because they are no longer orientals in the accepted sense of that term. They would feel as much out of place in Japan as we would. I know them, speak to them; I visit them and have them in my home, and I have not the slightest doubt that what I say is correct. If we are to avoid the troubles that other countries have had with racial minorities, then we must take a realistic view of the situation in British Columbia and attempt to make these people feel at home among us. We will secure their loyalty by fairness and kindness and by the practice of those other attributes which we exercise in our relations with other people.

But when the war came, the clamor against the Japanese Canadians prevailed over the few voices that appealed to reason. The Japanese Canadians were brought to Vancouver, where they remained until well into the spring of 1942, when they were removed to detention centers in the interior of the province. Their removal was not completed until the fall. By this time Japan's star was waning in the Pacific (the Battle of Midway, when the Japanese advance in the South Pacific was at last checked, took place on June 6, 1942). Yet evacuation continued, not only throughout 1942, but into 1943 and 1944.

In fact, the war provided the opportunity for disposing of the "problem" of the Japanese Canadians in British Columbia. In August 1944, the government of Canada decided that they were to be removed from the province altogether, to be "repatriated" to Japan or dispersed throughout the country.

The government's intention was to revoke the citizenship of Canadians of Japanese origin and to deport them. Prime Minister Mackenzie King introduced three Orders-in-Council (passed on

December 15, 1945) to implement this policy, a policy entailing the deportation of loyal citizens. "May I say that we have sought to deal with [this problem] and in doing so we have followed that ancient precept of doing justly but also loving mercy," he said, "and the Orders-in-Council . . . will give expression to that approach." King's gift for banality remained undiminished throughout his life.

The Orders-in-Council were racist. That is a word perhaps too often used nowadays, but we can understand its true meaning and the danger it represents by reference to the case of the Japanese Canadians. A group was singled out, solely on the ground that its members were of a different race than the majority, and subjected to cruel and degrading laws—even to the extent of denying them their citizenship. King wrote in his diary, after Hiroshima, that it was "fortunate that the use of the [atomic] bomb should have been upon the Japanese rather than upon the white races of Europe."

At last there were protests against the government's policy, and these soon spread throughout the country. On January 24, 1947, King gave in to them. He announced that the government would not carry out its deportation program. But by this time almost four thousand evacuees—half of them born in Canada—had left voluntarily for Japan. No doubt many who finally went would have remained in Canada instead of traveling to the bleakness of postwar Japan if the years of discrimination, the evacuation, and the confiscation of their property had not embittered them until they had no faith in Canada and no reason to stay.

By 1949, four years after the war had ended, the network of discriminatory legislation erected over the years by the federal and provincial governments had been dismantled. The Japanese Canadians were free at last to take their rightful place in Canadian life.

Since that time the racial virus has been kept in check in Canada. There has been no attempt in any province to erect a network of discriminatory laws and regulations. There are human-rights commissions at the federal level and in every province, and now, in addition, there are the provisions of the Charter of Rights. These give minorities the confidence to speak out, to protest the violation of their freedom, and to assert their claim to rights we have been taught we all should enjoy.

The equality guarantees of the Charter of Rights are not, of course, complete guarantees. There is the *non obstante* clause, which reserves to Parliament and the provinces the power to declare that a statute shall operate notwithstanding the Charter provisions relating to racial equality. They can only exercise this power, however, by an express declaration that the Charter guarantees are being set aside. Even when legislation is not accompanied by such a declaration, the Charter may still have to yield to it because the Charter also says that the rights set out in it are subject to "such reasonable limits prescribed by law as can be demonstrably justified in a free and democratic society." When may such reasonable limits be imposed on the right of a racial minority to the equal protection of the law? I suppose the answer is that it may be done when a majority in Parliament or any of the legislatures imposes such a limitation and the courts find such action to be demonstrably justifiable. Notwithstanding these deficiencies, there is in the Charter explicit recognition of the right of racial minorities to equality under the law. No one can say what the legal impact of this provision will be, but it stands as a symbol of Canada's commitment to multiculturalism in the fullest sense of the word.

The Constitution, the Charter of Rights, and the law do not, however, provide complete protection for racial minorities. It would be difficult to draft an instrument that did. Equality for racial minorities depends, in the end, on the attitudes of the citizenry. But we have progressed. The trial and torment of the Japanese Canadians have taught us something about the obligations of citizenship. In British Columbia, legislators used to strive to devise statutes that would limit the rights of racial minorities. In 1981, however, the legislature of British Columbia passed the Civil Rights Protection Act to combat racism by prohibiting racist propaganda. While the wisdom—and efficacy—of such legislation may be open to question, the change in public and legislative attitudes that it represents is important. Such legislation affirms society's commitment to racial equality.

The racism once made legitimate by political institutions is no longer legitimate, but as long as it finds a place in our collective psyche, it will constitute a threat, sometimes near, at other times far off, yet always present. Nothing is to be gained by pretending it does not exist, or by temporizing with evil. Each of us has an obligation to uphold the regime of tolerance. In *A Dream of Riches,* a book published by the Japanese Canadians' Centennial Committee in 1977, the Japanese Canadians expressed what should be the aspiration of us all:

> Having gained our freedom . . . we must not lose sight of our own experience of hatred and fear. Too often we have heard "damn Jew," "lazy Indian," from those who were once called "dirty Japs." The struggle of the generations and the meaning of the war years is completely betrayed if we are to go over to the side of the racist. Let us honour our history . . . by supporting the new immigrants and other minorities who now travel the road our people once travelled.

Let us now turn to an issue that in recent years has deeply engaged Canadians, the question of native rights. This takes us back to the beginning of Canada's history, to one race's occupation of a continent that was already inhabited by another race, which had its own culture, its own languages, its own religion, its own way of life. The issue of native rights is the oldest question of human rights in Canada and at the same time it is the most recent—for it is only in the last decade that it has entered our consciousness and our political bloodstream. In that decade, however, Canadian federalism has found it possible to embrace an expanding concept of native rights.

This has happened because the native peoples believed that their future lay in the assertion of their own common identity, and because the defense of their own common interests proved stronger than any had realized. When the suit brought by the Nishga Tribal Council of British Columbia to establish their aboriginal title reached the Supreme Court of Canada in 1973, all six judges who addressed the question supported the view that the Nishgas' title had been recognized by English law in force in British Columbia at the time of the coming of the white man. There is, in the judgment of Mr. Justice Emmett Hall in the *Nishga* case, that sense of humanity—that stretch of the mind and heart—that enabled the Court to look at the idea of native claims and to see it as the native people see it. This, of course, required some idea of the place of native history in Canadian history. It had been said in the lower courts that the Nishgas were, at the time of contact, a primitive people "with few of the institutions of civilized society, and none at all of our notions of private property." Mr. Justice Hall rejected this approach:

> The assessment and interpretation of the historical documents and enactments tendered in evidence must be approached in the light of present-day research and knowledge disregarding ancient concepts formulated when understanding of the customs and culture of our original people was rudimentary and incomplete and when they were thought to be wholly without cohesion, laws or culture, in effect a subhuman species. This concept of the original inhabitants of America led Chief Justice Marshall in his otherwise enlightened judgement in *Johnson* vs. *McIntosh* (1823) 8 Wheaton 543, which is the outstanding judicial pronouncement on the subject of Indian rights, to say: "But the tribes of Indians inhabiting this country were fierce savages whose occupation was war. . . ." We now know that that assessment was ill-founded. The Indians did in fact at times engage in some tribal wars but war was not their vocation and it can be said that their preoccupation with war pales into insignificance when compared to the religious and dynastic wars of "civilized" Europe of the 16th and 17th centuries.

Mr. Justice Hall concluded that the Nishgas had their own concept of aboriginal title before the coming of the white race and were entitled to assert it today:

> What emerges from the . . . evidence is that the Nishgas in fact are and were from time immemorial a distinctive cultural entity with concepts of ownership indigenous to their culture and capable of articulation under the common law having "developed their cultures to higher peaks in many respects than in any other part of the continent north of Mexico."

Thomas R. Berger

In January 1981, all parties in the House of Commons agreed that aboriginal rights of the native peoples should, together with their treaty rights, be entrenched in the Constitution. This provision is now a part of the new Constitution, albeit with the qualification that recognition is limited to "existing rights."

The entrenchment of the rights of the native people is thought by some to be anomalous. Why should they have any rights not enjoyed by other Canadians? To provide a formal place within the Constitution for aboriginal peoples is said to be an affront to the conventions of liberal democracy. Yet we have taken an irrevocable step here too, acknowledging at last what the native peoples have said all along, that they have the right to a distinct and contemporary place in Canadian life.

The recognition of such "anomalies" may in time constitute Canada's principal contribution to the legal and political order. Constitutional protection of French and English negates the idea of a monolithic culture. The guarantees to the Indians, the Inuit, and the Metis exemplify the Canadian belief in diversity. In this way the interests of the two linguistic communities and of the aboriginal peoples merge with the idea of multiculturalism.

The question of minority rights is also a question of the health of the body politic. Minorities make a positive contribution, indeed an indispensable contribution to the life of the nation. Dr. Ralf Dahrendorf, director of the London School of Economics, speaking in Toronto at Atkinson College, York University, on September 29, 1979, said:

> What is . . . surprising is that modern societies with their opportunities of affluence, their experience of terror, their values of citizenship rights and the rule of law still seek that homogeneity which breeds boredom and kills creativity. What is behind this desire today? Why is it that people seem to find it difficult, at the end of the twentieth century, to live with others who differ from them in language, culture, religion, colour?

The French-Canadian identity and culture may not survive in the redoubts of Anglophone dominance, but it will be a diminished Canada that denies French-Canadian minorities the opportunity to survive and to flourish. The rights of racial and ethnic minorities may be curtailed, but it will be a fearful and irresolute people who curtail them. We may reject the claims of the native peoples, but if we do we will be turning our backs against the truth of our own beginnings as a nation.

There is an idea of Canada that recurs in our history—an idea that speaks to us today, which tells us what Canada has to say to the world. Canadians are the heirs of two great European civilizations. There is the legacy from England of parliamentary institutions and the common law, and the egalitarian ideals and the notions of the rights of man derived from France. May we not erect on the structure of freedom bequeathed to us a regime of tolerance in which the place of minorities is secure? As we look at the condition of minorities around the world, it is clear that the issue of minority rights is the preeminent issue of our time. In Canada it is our commitment to diversity and our respect for the rights of minorities that evokes all that is best in the Canadian tradition.

What could be more relevant to the contemporary world? Everywhere, and within every nation-state, there are peoples who will not be assimilated and whose fierce wish to retain their common identity is intensifying as industry, technology, and communications forge a larger and larger mass culture, extruding diversity.

The Charter of Rights does not resolve the great questions of human rights and fundamental freedoms. In a sense they can never be resolved. They will continue to be the subject of inquiry, debate, and controversy. This will be a disappointment to those who crave certainty in these matters, who wish for a small world in which no one challenges prevailing certitudes, or who prefer to adopt a formula that reveals the necessary outcome of present confusion.

But the Charter of Rights will offer minorities a place to stand, ground to defend, and the means for others to come to their aid. The Charter is a landmark on the Canadian journey. That journey is a journey toward the regime of tolerance that Laurier dreamed of, toward a nation—and a world—where diversity is regarded not with suspicion but as a cause for celebration.

Gérald Godin

Quebec: The Language Question

Nine years after the passage of Bill 101 (1977), the law that made French the official language of Quebec, Quebecers are once again at the crossroads, and the language question still remains relevant.

Why? Compare two children born on the same day in Montreal. The child whose parents speak English will never in his life have to ask himself certain questions. He will never ask "Do the satellites roving the skies speak my language?" They do speak English. And the data banks being created by the large international organizations and the most powerful governments ever known in human history will speak English. And the video cassettes containing works, courses, the most up-to-date information in every field will speak English.

The global village that is only a step away, giving instant access from kitchens and living rooms to information of every type, to continuing education, and to all that constitutes the human heritage, will speak English.

The answer to this question for the French-speaking child in Quebec can only be "Perhaps." That is why he has to be able to count on someone somewhere to defend him, to make sure that he too will have ready access to the bank of human wisdom. In the case of small groups, it is the state that must assume this role and take action. If we members of small communities and small countries, trusting in others' respect for the rights of individuals, were to leave it to isolated individuals acting on their own to make contact in their own language with the global village, we would be shipwrecked and lost.

The individual rights of an English-speaking citizen of Quebec are preserved by the collective protection provided by the United States, a protection that follows from the United States' influence in the world. The collective responsibility is assumed by others who are all-powerful, and a young English-speaking Quebecer also has a good deal of time to devote his energies to defending his individual rights.

The young French-speaking Quebecer, on the other hand, does not have a Big Brother, and is treated somewhat disparagingly because he is less concerned about the rights of individuals. His priority is to find himself a Mini-Brother who will hold an umbrella over him to protect his brothers, sisters, parents, and, some day, his children.

This is what basically distinguishes the level of action of the two young Quebecers as well as the views they hold of the future, one in his native French, the other in his native English.

But why place so much weight on one's mother tongue? Because we shall never speak another language quite as well. We learned it from the lips of our mothers and fathers, and later at school, in the street, in books, from the poets and philosophers, from life itself in its infinite variety.

Anywhere in the world where there is more than one language group, the individual tongues fight one another. Each wants to survive, to expand, to take the other's place. The language groups are engaged in a perpetual cockfight.

Since common lore says that "language means jobs; language is money; language is prestige," language *is* money; it *is* jobs; it *is* prestige.

Therefore, Quebec decided to take action to guarantee the rights of its French-speaking community. We do not have an elephant, just a hundred miles away at Rock Island, who is concerned with protecting French.

Quite naturally, there have been some excesses and abuses, errors and offenses. Only the inhabitants of Utopia might believe that these changes, this revolution, could have come about in absolute calm and perfect harmony.

In the past, when anglicization was going on, there also were excesses and abuses, errors and offenses. They took place behind the doors of offices, factories, and conference rooms. They sometimes left a bitter taste or frustrations but no written proof, no newspaper articles illustrated by photographs of the "victims."

In those days the situation was diffuse, intangible, unexposable. Its scope and effects could be found only in the reports of Quebec's trade unions, the first to bell the cat. Other aspects were revealed in the work of the Laurendeau-Dunton Commission, the Gendron Commission, and so many other researchers since.

As a result of all this work, Quebec decided to act, returning French to first place in Quebec. Bill 101 corrected a situation that was slowly turning Quebec into a northern Louisiana.

Today, the language situation is being set right under the authority of Bill 101, an act that has empowered bodies who are responsible for its application and respect. Thus, there is an address, a door to knock on, and people to criticize. There is a place where discontent is focused, demonstrated, aired, and crystallized.

The present state of affairs is transparent; in the past it was opaque. Francization is going on in the light of day; it is well surrounded. In olden times, anglicization occurred out of public sight and hearing; it went unnoticed. Those who were subjected to it kept silent. Those who are the objects of today's francization do not go unnoticed. They show themselves in public. Their visible presence has created the impression that Quebec is going too far too fast, that it is insensitive to certain human truths.

Those who, in the past, were anglicized no longer feel the need to speak out. Those now being francized are given the support of many people, who, though in favor of francization, refuse to recognize that it is impossible to go from the anglicization of a majority to the francization of an administration and an economy without having to change and disrupt deeply rooted habits, attitudes, and traditions.

Anglicization hurts. So does francization. We had to make

a choice. There is no vacuum or no-man's-land in the field of language.

Moreover, by centralizing the discontent of those who have undergone francization, all society has gained because there is now a precise point for the start of dialogue, where communication can be open and criticism voiced. Out of this can and must come an improvement in the conditions under which francization takes place, takes its roots in reality, in the experiences of Quebec workers (and I use the word "workers" in its broadest sense).

A balance must be established between, on the one hand, the means open to the government of Quebec to maintain its cultural characteristics today, tomorrow, and even for the rest of time, as Pierre Perreault, the poet and film producer, would say, and, on the other hand, the type of protection provided for the rights of the English-speaking minority so that this minority will continue building Quebec, working closely with the majority. Finding this fine balance is no easy task.

Bill 101 is Quebec's third piece of language legislation. The first, Bill 63 (1968), protected the French and English languages, allowing freedom of choice. Bill 22 (1974) called French the official language and limited the earlier freedom of choice, barring the children of immigrants whose basic language was not already English from attending English-language schools. The legislation in Bill 101 is accompanied by a series of measures to ensure better participation in the very workings of the state by Quebec's cultural communities, including the English-speaking community. Furthermore, Bill 101 is being applied in the world of business and enterprise through negotiation. Not only is dialogue about the foundations of the bill being carried on, it is also being solicited, supported, and stimulated. In other words, the government is striving for transparency with its partners in the language question.

On the basic issue, French must be the language of work in Quebec. Otherwise, it is doomed to change from a language of bread, or *lingua del pane,* to a language of the heart, or *lingua del cuore,* as the Italians say. French must be conspicuous in office buildings, in companies, at work sites, in the places where the vast majority of Quebecers work. It must never revert to what it was in the days when Quebec's working men and women, office employees, secretaries, engineers, and researchers dropped their language in the cloakroom when they clocked in and picked it up in the evening as they went by what we used to call the "punch."

The great majority of firms respect and apply Bill 101. Here are a few statistics. The deadline prescribed for implementation of the language legislation, through special agreements and for certain firms, is 1990, thirteen years after the act was adopted. Now 87.6 percent of the larger companies either hold a certificate of francization or are carrying out programs to obtain certification. In small and medium-sized businesses, the percentage is 85.3 percent. In the case of organizations, we have reached 89.2 percent. A few more statistics reveal how many companies are already francized in the sense of the act. Of the 1,609 companies with a thousand employees or more, 400, or 25 percent, have their certificates. Of the 2,209 firms with a staff of fifty to ninety-nine, a certificate has been issued to 685, or 22 percent. The other firms are in the process of francization.

I would like to cite one example of francization and its effects. I have chosen the Compagnie Internationale de Papier plant at La Tuque because I have visited it and spent time with the firm's directors and employees. In the words of a La Tuque worker, "Twenty years ago, there were twenty-two Anglophones here, and the town's ten thousand citizens had to speak English. Those twenty-two people were the directors of the pulp and paper plants." And the situation now? French has become the language of work throughout the company's activities. The collective agreements are written in French. The internal communications and reports are in French. On the production machinery, fifteen thousand plates are still in English, but six thousand have already been translated. Why only six thousand? This question introduces the importance of terminology and terminology banks.

The firms that have joined together in an industrial association and the Office de la Langue française are now placing the finishing touches on a glossary of terms in the pulp and paper industry. This operation, which involves tens of thousands of words, is being carried out in cooperation with firms and language-research centers from other French-speaking countries. The right word must be chosen, and this word must be the same for the entire industry, regardless of where it is located in the French-speaking world.

The work in terminology and in determining the standard word is as important as the process of francization in the field. As soon as the standardization is completed, the machinery and the items in inventory will be identified in French.

The Compagnie Internationale de Papier plant at La Tuque is now 70 percent francized, and the entire industry is headed in the same direction.

For a good illustration of the extent of the operation, I offer two brief sketches of the new situation. The young workers entering the plant already work in French. It is the middle-aged workers who have to adapt, who have to forget their many years of working in English and their English vocabulary. In a sense, they have to relearn their own language in their own country. I asked one of them if he thought that Bill 101 was a good act, despite the extra burden that reclaiming his language represented for him and his fellow-workers of his age. "No, sir, it is not good," he answered. Then, after a long and disconcerting pause, he added, "It is essential."

Something still more promising, more significant, and more encouraging has occurred at the plant. The age of robots has arrived. Most of the operations are controlled and carried out in part by computers. And these computers speak French. This is what I would call phase two of the francization process.

What does the future have in store for Quebecers? Where will French be tomorrow? First of all, francization can only be accomplished if all Quebec citizens wish it, value it, and strive to achieve it. An operation of this scope can succeed only if it remains deeply rooted in the people who engendered it.

We should be aware that there may not be room for everyone at the great banquet of electronics, robotization, teleprocessing, and office automation. As a minority in North America, we are lucky to be in a small inn right next to the large hotel. We must be included now, with our language, our culture, and our imagination, in this wired and interconnected universe. There has to be a place for French in the twenty-first century.

What will we do with our place? The real issue, first and foremost, is that we have our say, that our uniqueness expresses itself and appears on the scene. And this uniqueness can, at times, allow itself to look very much like everyone else, so that its difference is not perceived. But the task will be to keep the door open to all possibilities, whatever their form. Thus, the question is not what we shall do with that liberty to be unique, but rather, how to keep it so that we can draw upon it.

If the small nations do not attend that future banquet to which progress is inviting us, all humanity will suffer. It will suffer since humanity has gone through the process of kings turning power over to citizens. History is now repeating itself; henceforth, we must be prepared for a world in which the equality of nations will be as important as the equality of citizens was in the past. On the global scale, the citizens are the nations.

We might have an elitist distribution of powers, that is, a distribution only among the large nations. In such a case, we would be subjected to the tyranny of a small number of strong nations concerning data-processing powers. Alternatively, there might be a democratic distribution of these powers that would take into account a respect for national sovereignties, be they large or small, and, in this case, there would be a place for each and every one.

All Quebecers are invited to face this task, especially the Anglophones who have chosen Quebec because they wish to participate in the challenge and because they believe that Quebec must maintain its uniqueness.

Some people might think me naive because I sincerely believe that the English of Quebec want to build a French Quebec, a French Quebec in which there must also be a place, a home, for everyone. Nonetheless, I continue to believe. And I believe because the time has come when we no longer argue about changing the name of Maple Street to rue des Erables somewhere in the Eastern Townships, but instead begin to work together to build a new Quebec.

Judy Erola

Women in the Eighties

I n Canada and in the United States, the women's movement is
currently confronting the challenge of translating its objectives into public policy. In both countries, this process of le-
gitimization, institutionalization, and politicization has been pro-
ceeding for the last thirty years within the traditional political
sphere.

It is an irrefutable fact that Canada has clearly benefited from
the work of feminist thinkers in the United States. Ideas of equality at the formal political level in Canada, however, have not been
as divisive, nor have they generated quite the hostility that they
have in America. The reasons are complex and lie embedded in the
substantial differences in Canadian and American political cultures, organizations, and institutions. What some feminist thinkers
might call "cooption by the system," I perceive as positive reaction
by government to the newly articulated needs of women.

In the United States, the "reborn" women's movement of the
1960s grew out of a volatile political climate that resulted in legislation to combat racial discrimination, legislation to clean up the
environment, and programs to combat poverty. Women achieved
notable policy successes in the very areas where the civil-rights
movement had made its greatest strides—in employment, educa-

tion, and legal equality. The gains were achieved with the passage of the Equal Pay Act in 1963, which was extended to government employees in 1964 and 1966; with Title VII of the 1964 Civil Rights Act; with the signing of Executive Order 11375 extending affirmative action to women in 1965; with the passage of Title IX of the education amendments in 1972; and with the passage by Congress of the Equal Rights Amendment in 1972. There was also a substantial reform of abortion laws by numerous states in the late sixties as well as the 1973 federal Supreme Court decision that made abortion legal throughout the country.

In Canada too, there has been a fairly long history of legislated equality rights. In 1956, at the federal level, there was the Female Employees Equal Pay Act, which was extended to public servants in 1971. Equal pay for work of equal value, or comparable value as it is known in the United States, became federal law in the Canadian Human Rights Act of 1978.

In some other areas, like affirmative action and contract compliance, Canada is only now moving to mandatory programs. The need for "special measures," however, has been recognized in human-rights legislation: the first Bill of Rights (1960), the federal contracts program of 1976, and the National Plan of Action (1979).

For Canadians, 1967 was a watershed, for it marked the inception of the Royal Commission on the Status of Women. Florence Bird, a well-known journalist and an American by birth who recently retired from the Canadian Senate, was appointed by Prime Minister Pearson and Cabinet to head the commission. The executive secretary of the commission was Monique Bégin, who later became a major figure in Prime Minister Trudeau's administration and an invaluable ally in the advancement of women's rights. The mandate of the commission was

> to inquire into and report upon the status of women in Canada, and to recommend what steps might be taken by the Federal Government to ensure for women equal opportunities with men in all aspects of Canadian society. . . . to inquire into and report on:
> 1. Laws and practices under federal jurisdiction concerning the political rights of women;
> 2. The present and potential role of women in the Canadian La-

bour force, including the special problems of married women in employment and measures that might be taken under federal jurisdiction to help in meeting them;

3. Measures that might be taken under federal jurisdiction to permit the better use of the skills and education of women, including the special re-training requirements of married women who wish to re-enter professional or skilled employment;

4. Federal Labour laws and regulations in their application to women;

5. Laws, practices and policies concerning the employment and promotion of women in the Federal Civil Service, by Federal Crown Corporations and by Federal Agencies;

6. Federal taxation pertaining to women;

7. Marriage and divorce;

8. The position of women under the Criminal Law;

9. Immigration and citizenship laws, policies and practices with respect to women;

and such other matters in relation to the status of women in Canada as may appear to the Commissioners to be relevant.

The Royal Commission went to the grass roots. Four hundred and sixty-eight briefs from organizations and individuals and about a thousand letters of opinion were received. There were public hearings in fourteen cities in all ten provinces as well as in the Yukon and the Northwest Territories. Eight hundred and ninety witnesses appeared before the commission. In several cities a "hot line" telephone service was set up so that people unable to come to the hearings could talk directly to a commissioner. An extensive program of research, including forty special studies, was undertaken. The findings constitute background for the commission's report.

The report of the Royal Commission on the Status of Women, submitted in 1970, included 167 recommendations, and more than two-thirds have been implemented. As in the United States, removing legal discriminations came first; changes in economic structures, that is, measures to improve women's economic position, take much longer.

The report has meant more to the status of women in Canada than is implied by its recommendations. The "sum" of the commission has indeed been greater than its parts, for the Royal Commission gave rise to government institutions—mostly at the federal level, but increasingly at the provincial level—that have been charged with placing women's issues on the government agenda. When so placed, they are visible, and attention must be paid!

The report was tabled in Parliament on September 20, 1970. In 1971, Prime Minister Trudeau appointed the first Minister Responsible for the Status of Women. The appointment was intended to ensure detailed governmental review and implementation of the Royal Commission recommendations. A senior official was appointed as coordinator for the Status of Women. This was the embryo of what is today Status of Women Canada, not legally defined as a government department, but constituted as an agency or secretariat.

Status of Women Canada reviews new legislation and new policies going forward to Cabinet, and works with other departments to coordinate new initiatives. In 1976, when Status of Women Canada was created as a separate agency, a directive was adopted by Cabinet requiring ministers to indicate clearly the impact of policy proposals on women. The directive does not work perfectly; unfortunately, not all drafters of policy documents are feminists (at least not yet). But the directive is a useful tool for the Minister Responsible for the Status of Women.

In 1973, the Federal Advisory Council on the Status of Women was created to educate the public and to advise the government on issues of importance to women. Its primary function is to provide research. Recognition of its value is evident in a budget that has steadily increased over the last ten years, and that now stands at about four million dollars.

A unique program for women, begun in 1973 and directed by the federal government, is the Women's Programme within the Department of the Secretary of State. It provides grants, contributions, resource materials, and advice to both national and regional women's groups throughout Canada. The office has headquarters in Ottawa and also has a number of regional offices. The objective of the Programme is to increase women's participation in all areas of society and to assist groups working to promote institutional progress in the status of women.

The Programme's grants and contributions totaled more than fifteen million dollars in the fiscal year 1985–86. Examples of groups who have been assisted by the Programme are the National Action Committee on the Status of Women, an umbrella organization of more than two million women and two hundred and thirty women's organizations; the Canadian Congress on Learning Opportunities for Women, which studies educational and career opportunities for women; and the National Association of Women and the Law, which concerns itself with the implications of legislative change affecting women. All these groups are actively involved in lobbying governments for improvements to the status of women.

As Minister Responsible for the Status of Women, I saw the need to establish university chairs in women's studies in order to stimulate the required research that was so underdeveloped on the university level. Accordingly, in 1984, Secretary of State Serge Joyal and I created a federal program that was to result in the establishment of five chairs in women's studies distributed regionally throughout the country. A committee of academics and government representatives was formed to screen applications from universities and to make recommendations to Cabinet. Each chair was to receive a half-million dollars toward its establishment. The first chair was awarded to Mount Saint Vincent University in Halifax, Nova Scotia.

In 1977, as recommended by the Royal Commission on the Status of Women, the federal Human Rights Commission was established. There are a number of provisions in the Canadian Human Rights Act of particular significance to women: (1) discrimination on the basis of sex or marital status is prohibited; (2) discrimination in cases of pregnancy and childbirth will soon be prohibited; (3) sexual harassment will soon be prohibited; and (4) affirmative action programs are specifically permitted, and the commission may order such a program as part of a settlement. It is to be noted that inasmuch as this constitutes federal legislation, only 10 percent of the labor force—employees of the federal government and of federally regulated industries—is thereby protected. Since the early seventies, however, provinces have created similar human-rights legislation, although the protections offered are not nearly so comprehensive.

In 1979, the Cabinet adopted a five-year plan for policy review and implementation in a wide spectrum of areas under federal jurisdiction. It was Canada's contribution to the mid-decade United Nations Program of Action. Called "Towards Equality for Women," this series of Cabinet commitments also strengthens the hand of the Minister Responsible for the Status of Women.

A major success in the women's movement in Canada was the historic victory that resulted from an interlocked external and internal women's lobby, the victory bringing women equality guarantees now enshrined in Section 28 of the new Canadian Constitution and Charter of Rights. This particular section is effectively the equivalent of the American Equal Rights Amendment, which would have become the twenty-seventh American constitutional amendment.

The question presents itself: Why could this legislation happen in Canada so much more easily than in the United States? In Canada, women's issues, equality issues, were taken to the federal government's heart due to the Royal Commission on the Status of Women. In fact, the Royal Commission made it impossible for any Canadian politician to oppose equality. That does not mean that all issues will meet with equal acceptance, but on the major idea that *there must be equality,* there is no political disagreement.

Let me now describe, from my perspective as Minister Responsible for the Status of Women, what actually happened in Canada—that is, the saga of Section 28. Canada's Constitution consisted of a number of acts of the British and Canadian parliaments, as well as unwritten conventions that have developed over the years. Its cornerstone is the British North America Act of 1867. Britain agreed to patriate the British North America Act if requested to do so by the Canadian Parliament with the concurrence of the provinces. It was Canada that had maintained the tie to Britain, for the federal government and the provinces could never agree to an amending formula that would provide for patriation. Conference after conference of prime ministers and premiers of the provinces dealing with the subject of patriation had ended in failure.

In 1980, the federal government decided to act unilaterally, that is, without provincial agreement. Prime Minister Trudeau presented the first draft of a new constitution to the Parliament of Canada, with an entrenched Charter of Rights and an amending formula. It was sent to a joint committee of both the House of Commons and the Senate, which called for briefs and public hearings. The joint committee, which sat for fifty-seven days, received submissions from 914 individuals and more than three hundred groups, including many women's groups.

Three important briefs were presented by the Canadian Advisory Council on the Status of Women, the National Action Committee on the Status of Women, and the National Association of Women and the Law. During the public hearings, these briefs were brilliantly defended by the witnesses, young women lawyers, who argued that the proposed charter of rights entrenching the equal rights of men and women did not go far enough. In January 1981, amendments that embodied some of their proposals were recommended to the joint committee by the Minister of Justice, Jean Chrétien. But an unequivocal statement of equality was, as yet, not forthcoming.

Consequently, a hastily formed ad hoc conference, attended by more than a thousand women, was held in Ottawa. The conference was followed by concerted lobbying. There were letters to and meetings with ministers and senators. Women contacted the media, took to the hustings, and called public meetings throughout the country.

In April, after two months of intensive lobbying, the Minister of Justice introduced into Parliament a new draft, which included Section 28, and the draft was passed unanimously by both houses. Three provinces, Saskatchewan, Alberta, and British Columbia, however, challenged in the courts the federal government's unilateral action. The case was argued in the Supreme Court in April 1981, and in September 1981, the Supreme Court ruled that the Canadian Parliament did have legal right to take the resolution to Britain in spite of the western provinces' opposition, although there was a convention that changes in the Constitution required "substantial agreement" by the provinces. And so the prime minister and the Cabinet, bowing to this convention, decided to return to the bargaining table.

The prime minister and the premiers of the provinces met in Ottawa on November 2-5, 1981. On November 5, Prime Minister Trudeau announced on television that nine of the ten provinces—the exception was Quebec—had agreed on an amending formula as well as on the Charter of Rights. There was, of course, no doubt that nine out of ten was a "substantial" consensus. It remained only for Parliament, both the House of Commons and the Senate, to give formal approval to the new draft before sending it to London.

Unfortunately, the new accord contained a rider giving the provinces the power to override certain rights set out in the Charter. The provincial governments could, by virtue of this provision, declare that certain legislation would operate notwithstanding the Charter. The effect of the rider could have been to render Section 28 inoperative.

As Minister Responsible for the Status of Women, I had three choices: to accept the "consensus" decision; to resign; or to find a way to convince the premiers of the provinces that the provincial override provision must be withdrawn. Opting for the last and counting on the unqualified support of the women of Canada, I informed the prime minister that I would rally the necessary troops and convince the premiers that their power to override was totally unacceptable. The prime minister was more than a little astonished—indeed annoyed—at my suggestion that this be done. He hastened to point out that the consensus that had been reached had his endorsement and, therefore, carried with it the support of Cabinet. My protest would be seen as a breach of Cabinet solidarity. Nonetheless, after a difficult and heated discussion, I managed to convince the prime minister that my role would be discreet, that I would *not* make a public statement, and that the women of Canada would move the premiers of the provinces to a new understanding of the situation. So, with a wink from the prime minister, I drew a deep breath, then plunged into a two-week battle that would have to be successful if my political career was to continue.

And so it was back to the trenches. Every woman member of Parliament and Senator was summoned to battle. My office telephones were coopted by the women's lobby to garner support in the provinces and across the country. I cajoled, badgered, flattered, insulted my Cabinet colleagues, but I did not cry!

The press had a field day with an excellent story. Journalists, male and female, provided national coverage of all the issues, and credit must be given to some of the top women journalists in Canada. They detected my pivotal role, but, understanding the importance of the issue and the sensitivity of my own Cabinet position, they did not divulge, early in the proceedings, my personal involvement.

One by one, the premiers of the provinces fell; they agreed to exclude Section 28 from the provisions of the override clause. On the evening of November 23, the last premier finally capitulated. The Minister of Justice walked into the House of Commons, and announced that he had the agreement of all the premiers. Section 28 was to be unequivocal after all. The section reads simply: "Notwithstanding anything in this Charter, the rights and freedoms referred to in it are guaranteed equally to male and female persons." I may add that the champagne flowed freely in my office that night.

The American Equal Rights Amendment is almost the equivalent of the Canadian Section 28, for the American amendment reads: "Equality of rights under the law shall not be denied or abridged by the U.S.A. or by any State on account of sex." It is regrettable that this amendment's time has not come, for, despite wide public support, political resistance proved inexorable. But, I am convinced, its time will come. As Katherine Mansfield said, "Regret is an appalling waste of energy; you can't build on it; it's only good for wallowing in."

It would be safe to say that the experience in both Canada and the United States has brought women political savvy. The lessons learned are that women must become more politicized; they must learn to play political hardball; they must elect more women to political office at all levels of government; they must send competent, diligent, and eloquent women into the "corridors of power."

Lord Acton said "power corrupts," but Gloria Steinem coined the feminist version: "It's not that women are less corruptible than men; it's that women have had less chance to be corrupt." The truth is that women have had precious little opportunity to test their moral fiber. Women must, and will, achieve more equitable representation.

And now that Canadian women have achieved constitutional equality, how do they reach economic security and independence? One Canadian columnist writing on this subject stated that "independent means leads to independent thinking." It is a fact that, notwithstanding legal guarantees, economic difficulties remain with women in the eighties.

Participation rates of women in the labor force in Canada and in the United States are similar: 52 percent of Canadian women over fifteen years of age and 53 percent of American women over sixteen. In both countries, participation rates are even higher among married women with children. In Canada, 55 percent of married women with children under sixteen are in the labor force; in the United States, the figure is 56 percent of married women with children under eighteen.

Labor-force projections prepared in both countries predict marked increases. A recent report released by the Canadian Task Force on Labor Market Development projected that 60 percent of women over twenty years of age would be in the work force by 1991. The study also concluded that adult women would account for almost two-thirds of the growth of the labor force through the eighties and that married women with children would be the fastest growing sector. Labor-force projections prepared by the United States Bureau of Labor Statistics indicate that women in the labor force will reach between 56.4 percent as a low estimate and 63.2 percent as a high estimate by the year 1990. In both countries, women remain concentrated in a narrow range of clerical, sales, and service occupations. These three occupational categories account for more than 60 percent of all employed women in both Canada and the United States.

One major consequence of women's concentration in a limited number of low-paying "women's jobs" is evident when the annual earnings of men and women are compared. In Canada, in 1980, the average woman working year-round earned 59 percent of what the average man earned. Furthermore, women's earnings were lower than those of men in all occupational groups, even in occupations in which women predominated. In the United States, the figures are calculated on a slightly different basis, but they still show women to be at a severe disadvantage. The median annual earnings of American women who worked full time for an entire year in 1980 was 60 percent of the median earnings of American men. Such statistics mean that policies must change.

Current employment policies must be examined from the perspective that most women, particularly women with children, are going to be in the labor force. These women will need better access to quality child care. The tax system must deal sensibly with the large outlays families make for such care. Support systems must be provided to the families that exist, not to the dream families from grade-school textbooks that may never have existed.

Good child care, reasonable maternity benefits, sensible tax laws do not destroy the family; to the contrary, they strengthen it. And women's economic independence will mean marriages of equality, not of dependency.

Canada is working for pension reform, a current concern in the United States too. When the Canadian government issued its "Green Paper on Pensions" in 1983, a special supplement, "Focus on Women," was also produced. As Canadians and Americans look to the end of the century and indeed to the aging of their populations, changes in pensions, public and private, are crucial, especially for women.

Young girls still shortchange themselves by dreaming dreams of knights on white horses who will take care of them forever. In high school such is still too often the focus, though it is certainly not the reality. Marriages do end in divorce—in Canada 40 percent of the time—and the result is that women are too often reduced to poverty.

The Royal Commission on the Status of Women was surprised

by its finding that women are more likely than men to be poor. A Royal Commission on Poverty, reporting at about the same time, did not even make this link. Improving women's economic status will reduce the likelihood of women spending their lives in poverty, and ending them in poverty. But it is evident that this world of real equality is not imminent; it is not around the corner.

Nevertheless, there are bright signs; all is not doom and gloom. There have been achievements. A major one has been the initial success in the area of serious study by Canadian legislators of family violence. The question of family violence appears on the negotiating agendas of federal and provincial ministers who have responsibilities either in the area of administration of justice or in the development of services.

There is further achievement in that more young women are in the professions. There are more women going into business, and they are succeeding. There are more women in nontraditional trades. There are more women entering politics and taking leadership positions—in the backrooms, in the legislatures, in Cabinet. Like Americans, Canadians have their first woman on the Supreme Court, Madame Justice Bertha Wilson. The Speaker of the House of Commons was a woman, Jeanne Sauvé, who became the present governor-general. The president of the Liberal party is a woman, Iona Campagnolo, who is also the chair of that party's policy committee.

Internationally, Canada has a fine track record of compliance with United Nations conventions. For example, the Royal Commission on the Status of Women prepared its report with reference to the Universal Declaration of Human Rights. Canada is an active force in the two major standing units within the United Nations concerned with the status of women issues in the widest sense: the Committee on the Status of Women and the Committee Concerned with the Convention on the Elimination of Discrimination against Women. Canada recently ratified this latter convention, one of five Western nations to do so. The United States, unfortunately, did not.

In the constellation of member states at the United Nations, Canada and the United States are undoubtedly among the fortunate, for Canadians and Americans live in countries of material affluence and wealth. When they contemplate the international scene, it is obvious that their vantage is one of privilege. There is, therefore, all the more reason for both countries to be in the forefront of change—of challenging entrenched inequities and of providing leadership in achieving the stated goals of equality.

H. Ian Macdonald

The Economy, Technology, and Innovation

T he Canadian view of United States economic policy is that it threatens the restructuring of the economy in Canada. Restructuring, though a horrible word, is a national imperative.

Fiscal expansion in the United States is largely investment based and related to technological development in the military, space, and health industries. For example, the United States Department of Defense alone spent roughly $38 billion on research and development in 1984–85, compared to about $7 billion spent by Canada for all its research and development, military and nonmilitary together. American spending, however, is so broad and so much higher than the pool of savings available to the government that it must draw upon financing from abroad. The result is that Canadians and Europeans have been funding American fiscal excesses with their own savings at a time when their money would be better spent on the restructuring necessary to improve productivity and reduce unemployment. Furthermore, because of poor corporate profitability and stop-go economic growth, savings in Canada and Europe are relatively scant. Thus, capital outflows to the United States have presented a problem for other countries which has been offset only partly by increased exports to the United States. The prospect of increased protectionism can only exacerbate this problem.

Thus, from an outsider's perspective, the American strategy appears to be, first, to borrow from abroad to create a host of new technology industries; and then to pay for these foreign debts with the very technological goods and services that those debts have brought into being. This strategy is driven by American concern and fear in the face of Japan's rapid emergence in technology and by Japan's ability to isolate its capital markets from international capital flows. In other words, Japan has not paid for American fiscal imbalances as other nations have.

Meanwhile, what effect has this strategy had on Canada? It has forced Canadians into a defensive posture on economic policy so that concern in Canada is more closely focused on the exchange rate and its link to inflation than on growth. Being forced into such a policy stance is particularly inappropriate and frustrating when over a million Canadians, many of them young, are out of work.

Unemployment rates in Canada are not only higher than in the United States, but they also have been rising lately while American unemployment rates have been falling. The rate in Canada fluctuates at about 3 to 3.5 percent higher than it does in America. Canadians look upon unemployment as a national calamity and its reduction as their most urgent priority. What Canadians require is higher investment in education and innovation, with the ultimate goals, through such investment, of higher productivity and job creation with economic renewal. Those goals, however, are impeded by Canada's multifaceted dilemma: American economic policy is drawing upon Canadian savings; it is causing disquiet in Canadian financial markets; this, in turn, is distracting Canadian policy makers from acting upon their pressing priorities of job creation and the formation of new firms. American policy also threatens to leave Canadian industry behind in a technological dark age by the 1990s. This is a formidable dilemma—and from a Canadian perspective it is all the fault of the United States. If good fences make good neighbors, then perhaps Canadians should do something about that longest unguarded border in the world!

In IDEA Corporation (Innovation Development for Employment Advancement), an Ontario agency which I chair, Canada is working to encourage investment in the new technologies. Few investors in Ontario, however, are interested in the Canadian scene because investment opportunities in the United States are so attractive. Thus, the expansion of risk-capital in Ontario is limited, and, in turn, Canadian ability to finance new technology firms is also limited. This has led to a new concern, namely, the issue of continental markets and managing of multinationals.

Canada has initiated discussions on free trade in key industries, including infomatics, steel, mass transit, agricultural equipment, petrochemicals, and textiles. Canadian concern does not spring from successful past ventures in bilateral free-trade agreements; for example, the Auto Pact has resulted in trade deficits for Canada in more years than not. Rather, Canadians fear that American industry and Congress will harm Canadian interests in what seems to be a growing trend to protectionism of the American market. In most of the sectors where it has advocated free or liberalized trade, Canada has competitive technology and international marketing. For example, a counterpart corporation of IDEA Corporation, the UTDC (Urban Transit Development Corporation) has developed efficient and sophisticated mass transit systems, which it is now installing in Detroit and Boston. The Canadian steel industry is also competitive on an international scale.

It is, however, in the area of infomatics that there is, on a number of fronts, the greatest uncertainty and debate in Canada. What is infomatics? No one knows, precisely. The universe of infomatics products and services is potentially immense and could include telecommunications, computer manufacturing programs, data processing and services. In many of these commodities Canada is already trading virtually free of tariffs, while in others the domestic market is protected for cultural and sovereignty reasons.

Who manages infomatics? Like many sectors in Canada, a great deal of the bilateral trade is conducted by subsidiaries of American parent corporations. Thus many of the advantages for Canada of free trade are called into question—as they have been to some degree in the Auto Pact. Some observers fear, for example, that Canadian data processing would be done in the United States, leaving Canadian users as mere terminals. Others are concerned that the United States might control the flow of data and the sale of technology—in the wake of increasing interdependence between the two countries. These fears have some substantiation. Not long ago, Canada sought discussion with the United States about allegations that Canada might be "leaking" American-originated computer technology to the Soviets, in a general concern that the United States is influencing where and when Canadians can ship their products.

What is the record? Canada's balance of payments in technology, which is chiefly influenced by trade with the United States, continues to be in serious deficit. For every one hundred dollars of trade conducted in these products, Canada records a deficit of about thirty-three dollars. By comparison, American trade balance in technology has been both positive and growing. In view of these contrasts, many Canadians wonder what there is to gain in opening up the borders, and many see the infomatics option as the American quid pro quo for the other sectors.

Michael Pitfield, a Canadian senator and sometime civil servant interested in these matters, spoke with concern in 1984 on the general topic of expanding free trade, and I suspect his anxiety is most acute over the technological or infomatics field: "Surely we have had enough of such situations as the Auto Pact, the fisheries treaty and the Alaska pipeline where the vicissitudes of the American congressional system are used as justification for the American government backing out of its commitments or twisting our tail for further concessions. That is the oldest American bargaining tactic in the book and we are suckers if we fall for it." Those are strong words, and there is great consternation, which is not without foundation, about the emerging bilateral relationship in the technological era. Canada's true multinational technology firm, Northern Telecom, has created more jobs in the United States in the past four years than it has in Canada. This fact is an indication of the compellingly attractive and persuasive climate for technology that Americans have created in their country. Things in the United States are growing and moving, but above all they are adventuresome!

Most of the bilateral trade between Canada and the United

States is already tariff-free, and there are prospects for even broader liberalization. For the past ten years, the two major planks of Canadian industrial policy—the Federal Investment Review Agency and the National Energy Policy—have regulated corporate production and performance. Both have been challenged by the United States, and the Foreign Investment Review Agency has been superseded by Investment Canada, which is now attempting to dispel the negative perception of Canada as a destination for foreign direct investment.

As chairman of IDEA Corporation, I have come to understand first-hand the relevance of Canada's former regulation of industrial activity and the negative influence such measures can have on a country's ability to restructure itself. The Foreign Investment Review Agency was established to preserve Canadian ownership in secondary industry. Over the years, it had been strengthened or weakened according to the vicissitudes of public opinion, the economic cycle, and the need for foreign direct investment.

At the same time, the Foreign Investment Review Agency had a real influence on corporate acquisition in Canada. In exerting that influence, however, it suppressed investor interest in young technology firms and, I would argue, impeded Canadian efforts to restructure the economy. Venture capital provides both the American and the Canadian economies, in particular the American, with the initial means for launching young technology firms. Venture investors seek capital gains through the selling of equity to large corporations—indirectly on secondary stock markets, or directly by way of acquisitions. Any regulation that affects initial public offerings or corporate acquisition subsequently affects the capital gain potential of the venture capitalist. In Canada, equity markets are comparatively thin—particularly at the secondary level. As a result of the Foreign Investment Review Agency, Canada regulated corporate acquisition markets. Consequently, venture capital was inhibited, and the formation of young technology firms impeded.

With the change of government from the Liberals to the Progressive Conservatives in 1984, Canada established Investment Canada, which is responsible for implementing a policy openly favoring foreign direct investment by reducing both the scope and the rigor of foreign investment screening. Through such a policy, economic growth and new employment opportunities are being furthered as major goals in the restructuring of the Canadian economy.

Long-standing circumstances are partly to blame for the problems in this economic restructuring. Canada has a comparatively small, resource-based and largely foreign-controlled economy, which is technologically underdeveloped. As I stated, for every one hundred dollars of high technology products crossing the border, Canadians incur a deficit of about thirty-three dollars. Canadian spending on research and development, proportionate to national income, continues to lag seriously behind that of the country's major trading partners and countries of comparable size and industrial structure. The business sector in Canada conducts considerably less of its national research and development than business sectors in other countries. Perhaps of greatest concern is what the Economic Council of Canada has recently found—that Canadian industry is generally slow in adopting and adapting new products and processes even when the benefits of doing so are evident.

Meanwhile, the contribution of technology to Canada's economic welfare is daily more demonstrable. In I D E A Corporation, with its unique perspective on innovation and the marketplace, there is evidence in three ways of the importance of the growth of technology. First, Canada's high technology manufacturing industries led all other industries in the 1970s in rate of output, growth, productivity, and investment, and those industries had the lowest increases in prices. Second, Canada's balance of trade is increasingly determined by technology-intensive products and related services. For example, as a percentage of Canada's overall trade turnover, both its exports and imports, high technology items rose—in a significant shift—to 25 percent in 1981 from only 20 percent a decade earlier. Third, Canada is finding that new technology production, at least in its formative stage of development, is labor intensive and often well paying.

At the same time that Canada has home-grown impediments to the encouragement of innovation, balanced by clear evidence of the importance of growth in technology, it has, nevertheless, an impressive capability for technological advancement. Because they cannot afford to, federal and provincial governments are not stimulating a broader base of innovation. Budget deficits have ballooned in successive economic recessions, and tax incentives for research and development are already among the most generous in the OECD (Organization for Economic Cooperation and Development) countries. Indeed, in 1983 the federal budget and the Ontario provincial budget had supplementary papers arguing that, because of structural problems, further fiscal stimulus to research and development probably would not be cost effective. Canada has gone as far as, or further than, most in this direction.

What, then, are the constraints on Canada's technological capabilities? Although these policy statements on Canadian innovation have stirred little public debate, they seem to recognize that constraint is the result of rising costs of research and development, government debt, and high foreign ownership. In the latter, the problem is that research and development are concentrated in parent firms rather than in their Canadian subsidiaries. Canada has a high proportion of small- to medium-sized firms which are effective and efficient, but which lack funds for research and development. In addition, small defense expenditure keeps Canadian figures for research and development low in comparison with those in countries with military build-ups.

Thus, discussion of future technological capabilities in Canada might appear to have reached an impasse. Canada knows its shortcomings and understands the need to encourage and broaden innovation, but it finds no obvious place to develop its capacity.

These are the major obstacles to innovation that entrepreneurs, investors, and managers face in dealing with new technology in Canada. In smoothing the way for innovation, I would suggest four objectives: first, increase the amount of available pre-venture capital; second, strengthen the relationship between university research and industry; third, stabilize the economic climate for innovation; and fourth, improve the diffusion of new technology into industry.

In regard to the first objective, a long-standing issue in Canada has been the lack of risk-capital for technological innovation. Universities provide one of the principal sources of innovation, but risk-capital has not been available to them. Instead, research in Canadian universities is sponsored primarily by the federal government's granting councils, which normally finance research and development with no view to commercial application. Typically, two to four years of further development remain before that research can reach the marketplace. To the pre-venture capitalist outside the university, such long lead times create unacceptable risks.

The province of Ontario established IDEA Corporation to close these gaps between innovation and commercial development—in the words of the act, "to bring together the research capabilities of the public sector with the commercial and industrial sector." Thus the corporation funds major research projects in Ontario universities. For example, at Queen's University in Kingston, Dr. A. J. DeBold has discovered and purified a substance produced by the heart, which is a natural diuretic. With support from IDEA, he and his team are now working on developing the ability to produce the substance, which he calls cardionatrin, in commercial quantities. Also funded is research at the University of Western Ontario that will develop methods to synthesize a unique group of compounds for selectively depositing metal in electronic circuit manufacture.

Until recently, the federal government and universities conducted more than half of Canadian research and development— the highest proportion by far of public sector funding among major OECD countries. Canadian universities perform about 20 percent and finance about 10 percent of national research and development, only a small part of which is under contract to industry. Universities, therefore, play a key role and have a major influence in raising national levels of technology. Clearly, the needs of industry must combine with the capabilities of the university. An interrelationship can be built on three fronts: sponsored research; cross-pollination among the laboratory, the office, the drawing board, and the classroom; and the training of more entrepreneurs and the promotion of the entrepreneurial spirit.

In the competitive realities of the eighties, when technology increasingly influences national output and employment, there can be no question that partnerships between the universities and industry will serve effectively the needs of both. For instance, IDEA has provided a loan to RMS Industrial Controls, Inc., a British Columbia company that has been attracted to Ontario by the high quality of Ontario's university resources. In the expanded operations of RMS in Ontario, research in RF microwave thin film components will be facilitated by working with the universities.

Such an objective is critical enough to demand detailed assessments of how to structure and reorganize incentives to link the university to business. In the United Kingdom, for instance, policy makers are now considering a bonus provision within the university granting system whereby twenty-five cents is provided by the government for every dollar obtained in industrial contracts.

According to a 1983 study on high technology from the United States Department of Commerce, "innovative activity and the willingness to apply technological advances are directly and substantially affected by the general economic environment and government macroeconomic policies." A recent poll of Canadian high technology firms reflects the same principle: a more favorable economic climate is identified as the first priority for innovation development.

In short, the third objective of improving the rate of private sector capital formation—that of stabilizing the economic climate for innovation—will, in turn, advance innovation. Economic policy for the mid-eighties must make this objective a priority because the capital demands of governments in Canada threaten to drain the pool of savings available for productive investments. At the same time, higher productivity from new process technology will allow greater repatriation potential in the large number of American-owned firms in Canada. With the prospect of such an increased mobility of capital internationally, Canada must ensure that its economy is attractive to long-term investment.

In regard to the improved diffusion of new technology in existing industry, a recent study by the Economic Council of Canada found that small- and medium-sized firms in Canada are generally slow in grasping new production technologies. The reasons for slow diffusion are the difficulties in obtaining information on new techniques, in applying these techniques to the plant, and in financing the conversion of production. Ontario has recognized the importance of technology diffusion; six technology centers are now advising firms on new production processes. Furthermore, part of the mandate at IDEA is to contribute to public education, and IDEA is taking on a substantial role in public policy development and is educating industry about the needs and opportunities of technological innovation.

Perhaps the most important point to recognize is that the achievement of a higher level of technological innovation in Canada will not happen overnight. The real task is to approach the frontier of economic growth, knowing that the encouragement of innovation and the application of technology is a long and difficult process.

Canadians have a tough job ahead of them, yet my view is steadily optimistic. With the assistance of agencies such as IDEA Corporation and an attempt to implement the four objectives I have outlined, Canada can and will control its progress into the future. Indeed, many of the problems are now being addressed, and by the time Canada has been fully won over by technology, Canadians will find that they have created, in Canada, more competitive and efficient industries, with new challenges for economic and technological progress in the future.

Let me end by expressing the spirit of Canadian/American differences in another way. Canada left the bosom of the British Empire and formed a nation, only to be tightly embraced, economically and culturally, by the United States, its closest neighbor. Canadians often wonder whether the American embrace, as I have shown it in the economic sense, has changed from the hug of a friendly neighbor to the unwitting stranglehold of a domesticated bear! (Indeed, more recently, the American hug has been compared to that of a grizzly bear!) It is because Canadians are inextricably tied to Americans in a number of ways that we wish to emphasize our differences so that we will not disappear altogether.

A fiercely Canadian friend recently told me that one of her American in-laws, wishing to give her a warm compliment, hugged her and said: "You don't seem like a Canadian at all. You could come from Boston—or even New York!" She did not take offense, though she was amused. The American in-law meant that my friend did not conform to the stereotypical view of a Canadian as a sensible, worthy, stodgy sort of person not given to self-dramatization. But in actuality, as Charles Ritchie, the Canadian ambassador, has pointed out: "Our most successful act as Canadians has been to put over on others the impression of ourselves as uncomplicated." Of course, a virtuoso performance of the uncomplicated Canadian has been given to North America by Bob and Doug McKenzie, and they are doubly hilarious to Canadians because of the strong irony with which they portray that image.

There is one final symbol of Canadian pride and Canadian difference that is anything but uncomplicated. Terry Fox was the first modern Canadian hero. He had lost one of his legs to cancer, and, in 1980, in order to raise money for cancer research, he decided to run across the vast land of Canada from coast to coast, in what he called his "Marathon of Hope." With an artificial limb, a lot of training, and a stubborn refusal to recognize the enormous odds against him, he began his run in Newfoundland. There is not a Canadian alive whose heart and imagination were not captured by the incredible courage—and pigheadedness—of what Terry Fox was trying to do.

Canada's biggest natural disadvantage is the sheer vastness of its land mass. Survival for Canadians has always been associated with survival against an impossible geography. Yet a one-legged man decided that he was going to conquer that vast expanse, to fight his own cancer and that of millions of others by raising research funds, and to unite his fractious nation with its regionalist attitudes —by simply running across it.

Terry Fox made it to Thunder Bay, Ontario—almost half-way across Canada—when cancer invaded the rest of his body. He was taken home to British Columbia where he died shortly afterward. He was defeated by the land; he was defeated by cancer—but to Canadians, he is one of the greatest winners and the noblest heroes in Canadian history. It is not a matter of sentimentality or tragedy. It is a matter of the definition of what it is to win. Because

Canada is a small nation spread out across a monstrous land, Canadians do not hope or want to win in the way that Americans win, because they cannot. Consequently, with a balance of Canadian pragmatism and idealism, Canadians have redefined what it is to win. Terry Fox's decision to run his "Marathon of Hope" was, consciously or unconsciously, very shrewd in the way Canadians have always been shrewd. Despite his breathtaking hope, he must have known he would not complete the run, and it is precisely that knowledge, combined with his recalcitrance in the face of it, that makes him a specifically Canadian hero.

One of Leonard Cohen's novels is entitled *Beautiful Losers*. That is an American-minded title, and an American-minded person might see Terry Fox as the most beautiful of losers. But to Canadians, he is a symbol of how Canadians have to live and work against formidable odds caused by circumstances beyond their control that are unique to Canada. The Canadian way is not to expect to beat these odds, which are given and immutable, but to concede to them in the noblest possible way, and through such concession, or compromise, to win—at the highest level. (Terry Fox attracted so much money for cancer research that there was a problem, at first, in its sheer administration.)

In working against great difficulty, the Canadian economy represents a typical Canadian problem. And until other Canadian heroes surface to inspire their country with a way of conceding yet winning, Canada—in terms of its economy—will press on with such strategies as I have suggested.

Bob Rae

A Three-Party System: Beyond the Politics of Tweedledum and Tweedledee

Observers of American politics have long been perplexed by the fact that the United States, alone among Western industrial democracies, has no real social democratic party. This fact has even been canonized into the doctrine of "American exceptionalism."

What follows is not another attempt to answer Werner Sombart's eighty-five-year-old conundrum, "Why is there no socialism in the United States?" Rather, this essay reflects the working and thinking of a social democratic politician in Canada on how and why a third party has thrived north of the forty-ninth parallel, concluding with some reflections on that party's prospects for the future.

I spent six years of my childhood in the United States. My father was in the diplomatic service, and I attended primary and junior high school in Washington, D. C. Like all good boys of that age, my brother and I had a newspaper route. We started with the *Washington Daily News,* then moved on to the *Star;* both papers are now out of existence. Two of the people on our route were quite famous. One of them, Richard Nixon, was, at that time, vice president, and the other, Estes Kefauver, a former candidate for the vice presidency, was then a very active senator. Every Christmas my brother and I would go around and ask our customers to buy a calendar. We managed to sell one to Richard Nixon. Mrs. Nixon was there, and she counted out ten pennies. Senator Kefauver was one of our customers who was never home to pay his bill, but one Christmas we did find him there. He was feeling the spirit of the occasion, and when he came to the door, he rummaged in his pocket, pulled out a twenty-dollar bill, and placed it in my hand. Ever since then, I have always felt closer to Democrats than to Republicans.

Some time later, when I was a federal member of Parliament, I was a member of the Canada-United States Interparliamentary Committee, which meets twice a year on both sides of the border. At one meeting I was seated next to a Republican senator. In a discussion of questions about housing and mortgage interest rates, he stopped in the middle of the conversation and said, "Son, you sound to me like some kind of socialist." It was with a state of shock that he then realized that there are, in fact, socialists elected to the House of Commons in Ottawa and to many legislatures in the provinces. Canada is not like the United States.

The existence of a viable, successful, and—dare I say it?—flourishing party of the democratic left in North America has its roots in three basic facts about Canada.

The first is the course of western radicalism and socialism in Canada. From the time of the settlement of the prairies, it became clear that a unique economic and political structure was developing in Canada's west. With the emergence of a grain economy in western Canada at the turn of this century, there was the quick rise of a farmers' movement, a graingrowers' cooperative movement, that came up against the large and eastern-Canadian institutions that dominated—then and now—the Canadian economy. These institutions were the banks, the railway companies, and the commercial interests that controlled the grain market.

It did not take long for the feeling of alienation to develop among a group of people who saw themselves in constant conflict with institutions and people who were almost uniquely central Canada, and this means primarily Toronto and Montreal in geographical terms, in orientation, and in outlook. Here was, then, the beginnings of an east-west conflict in Canada that persists to this day. This is a conflict that is central to an understanding of some of the political tensions within Canada, and also central to the emergence of Canada's third party, the New Democratic Party.

The New Democratic Party has been born at least twice. In 1933, the Co-operative Commonwealth Federation was born, the first electorally oriented expression of democratic socialism as a political force in Canada. The leadership and the majority of the support came from the western provinces. Later in the context of the 1958 landslide election victory of the Progressive Conservatives under John Diefenbaker and of the gradual convergence of the Co-operative Commonwealth Federation and the Ontario-based industrial unions, the party was born again in 1961 as the New Democratic Party.

Western radicalism and populism, therefore, are traditions in political thought and action that are fundamental to understanding the New Democratic Party today. These are the Party's roots. The Co-operative Commonwealth Federation was more than a movement; it was the government of the province of Saskatchewan in 1944, the first social democratic government in North America. This government lasted for nearly twenty years, and re-emerged as a New Democratic government until its defeat in 1982. The New Democratic Party has been the government in British Columbia as well, and continues in power today in Manitoba and the Yukon Territories.

Western radicalism and populism also gave rise to a very strong cooperative movement that remains strong in western Canada, particularly in British Columbia. Unlike central and eastern Canada, whose financial institutions are primarily banks and trust companies, western Canada continues today to consider the coop and the credit union as a strong second force in finance and commerce.

Western radicalism and populism in the United States, in marked contrast, were quickly taken over by established political forces. That is not something exclusive to the American west. The occasional wave outside the two-party system may rise, but none has ever managed to establish itself in the United States as a permanent force. In this century the Democratic and Republican parties have always managed to subsume, or coopt, and take on the color of whatever kind of protest movement arose. The protest of farmers, labor, women, or minorities in the United States did not give rise to the same kind of coherent ideology that occurred in Canada.

The labor movement is the second force that was central to the creation of a third-party movement in Canada. At the time of the great organizing drives of the American labor movement in the 1930s, the leadership of the industrial unions was imbued with very strong social democratic or democratic left ideals. The Reuther brothers, for example, were strong leaders with a close affinity to the ideas of social democracy. But the United States also had Franklin Delano Roosevelt, and the Democratic party forged the coalition with the progressive elements of the American labor movement that cut off any prospect of a third party.

The Democratic party was able to build such a coalition largely because of the frailty of socialist organizations to its left. This was its great opportunity and the great weakness of the alliance it forged. Without an established political force to his left, Roosevelt could take over a number of ideas associated with socialism without having to adopt socialist principles. And, of course, *pace* right-wing Republicans, what resulted was not socialism but an interventionist style of progressive liberalism. Later, when much of the American public began to reject progressive liberalism in favor of reactionary liberalism, the difference between the Roosevelt alliance and authentic socialism became clear. Increasingly, the Democratic party had nothing to offer except the well-worn formulas of earlier decades. In Canada, by contrast, the left-right swings of the two major political parties have always been constrained by the existence of a third party on the left, which, as a consequence, has also been able to have a real influence on governments, even though the third party has not yet formed a national government.

The same labor movement of the 1930s, the same members of the Congress of Industrial Organizations—autoworkers, steelworkers, packinghouse workers—had similar importance to the Canadian industrial belt as they did in the industrialized northeast of the United States. But whereas in the United States the leadership of these organizations had an effect on the nature of the Democratic party in states such as Pennsylvania, New York, and Ohio, the orientation in Canada was different. The leadership of the Canadian trade-union movement has maintained to this day its sense of independent radicalism. The fact that Canada had an established democratic left party meant that there has always been a socialist element in the labor movement and that Canadian trade unionism has not made the same compromises as its American counterpart in pursuing political influence.

The other difference between the Canadian and the American labor movements is the public sector. In the 1960s, the Canadian labor movement expanded enormously into the public sector to the degree that the largest union in Canada today is the Canadian Union of Public Employees, which has nearly three hundred thousand members. The leadership of this union, as with other public-sector unions, is oriented toward the New Democratic Party, as was the leadership of the industrial unions in the 1930s. In the United States, unlike almost every other country in the Western world, public-sector unionism has not been a major phenomenon. The United States today has fewer workers organized as a proportion of the labor force than virtually any other industrial democracy. By contrast, a Canadian worker is almost twice as likely to be a member of a trade union. The conservatism of American political culture is both reflected and nourished by that fact.

The third reason for the rise and the continuation of a third party in Canada is the parliamentary system. The party system in the United States is incomparably weaker than in Canada. American parties do not have much power or ability to control the behavior of their members, elected or nonelected. It is impossible to tell the difference between a conservative Democrat and a liberal Republican on the basis of their voting records in Congress. The emergence of political action committees with their enormously powerful financial resources has worked to undercut further the strength and cohesiveness of partisan-based discipline. And because of the logrolling way Congress works, the American political system confers a wide discretionary power on the individual member of Congress.

In Canada, the three-party system is very strong. The parliamentary system gives tremendous power to the executive. If one party holds a majority in Parliament—and, historically, one usually does—the members of the majority are expected to conform to the will of the executive. The ability of the patronage system to maintain loyalty within the party in power, the tantalizing whiff of the pork-barrel to the government-in-waiting, is strong enough to ensure little room for the kind of give-and-take seen daily in Congress.

The labor movement and the western farmers' movement discovered early that the only way to affect the political system was to create their own party, with all the loyalty and discipline required in Canadian terms. If people simply voted for one of the two old-line parties, the Liberals or the Conservatives, they could not control the behavior of those members. Ultimately, a Liberal or a Tory is a Liberal or a Tory, last and always.

I should add that, from the vantage point of someone who has been in the third party of a three-party system, I have cast the occasionally envious eye toward American legislators. The closest approximation in Canada to the American system is a minority government, even though it is during a minority government that party discipline assumes even greater importance. Minority governments in Canada have been among the most productive governments, despite their often shorter lives, because the imbalances of the "first-past-the-post" system are then somewhat compensated by the consensus making necessary to pass legislation and to ensure that governments survive.

Canadian and American political cultures, then, are different, and have produced different party systems. Social democracy is not a fringe movement in Canada. New Democrats have formed governments, and have often held the balance of power in minority situations. Equally important, the very existence of the New Democrats has forced the spectrum of political and social debate to the left. Liberals and Conservatives have borrowed much to keep the socialist hordes at bay. The lack of such a force in American politics has affected what is even allowed on the political agenda.

But no political culture is stagnant; political traditions can change. Reaganism in the United States is forcing the Democratic party to examine its roots and its appeal and to build a new coalition. Socialist parties in Europe can take nothing for granted as they are challenged by the new liberalism and new radicalism of the Greens and the revival of centrist parties. In Canada it would be a foolish person indeed who would predict with any confidence the events of the next few months, let alone the decade ahead. Consumer politics have become more fickle and more volatile. Historical tradition may well be a less reliable guide than in the past.

Over the years, pundits have been proclaiming the death of the New Democratic Party. More recently, some observers have been declaring the same of the Liberal party. Both these accounts are exaggerated. But they do point to a fact about political life. It is a mistake to assume that patterns and habits of political behavior will persist simply because they have existed for a long time. Political dynasties have been swept away in the past, and will be again in the future, because of powerful underlying trends that are unnoticed until successful. The ancient Chinese had an expression to the effect that whoever tries to overthrow an emperor will be either a bandit or a future emperor. It all depends on what happens.

Just before the First World War, the British journalist George Dangerfield wrote a brilliant little book, *The Strange Death of Liberal England*. In 1906 Britain had witnessed the election of the largest Liberal majority in history, with great figures like Asquith and Churchill and Lloyd George in government. Five years later, the Liberal party was under siege. By the beginning of the 1920s, the Liberal party in Britain was a mere shell, and has never since formed a government. Labor unrest, Irish nationalism, the suffragette movement—basic social changes—combined to eat away at the foundations of the comfortable, nineteenth-century, mildly reformist view that was represented by the British Liberal party.

No doubt there are many Canadian journalists working late to produce the same book about the Canadian Liberal party, the party that, under Prime Ministers Laurier, Mackenzie King, St. Laurent, Pearson, and Trudeau, dominated national politics since the beginning of the twentieth century, and yet was reduced to a mere 40 out of 282 seats in the House of Commons in the federal election of September 1984.

The historical basis of the Liberal party as the governing party has been its ability to represent some kind of entente between the distinctive aspirations of Quebec and those of the rest of Canada, and its ability to occupy an all-encompassing middle ground on social and economic issues. Today we are seeing an erosion (I think this word gives some sense of the gradual wearing away of the old magic) of the Liberal party's *automatic* claims to national government, as New Democratic and Tory gains have recently shown. This erosion points the way at least to the possibility of a realignment in Canadian politics.

One of the profound differences between Canada and the United States is that the Canadian provinces have real power. They have control, for example, over resources, education, the delivery of social services, health care, and workers' compensation. To a much greater degree than the American states, the provinces are strong economic and social partners with the federal government. The Liberal party has failed to come to grips with the collapse of its own regional base because it has failed to understand that the power and the force of regionalism have become a vital fact of Canadian political life. Pierre Trudeau epitomizes that failure. His focus, his understanding, his reason for being in politics had to do with the role of Quebec in Canada and the role of French Canadians in the governing of the country. He accomplished many remarkable feats in those areas that concerned him most, but they came at tremendous cost. For example, he was blind to the sense of alienation in the west, and that hurt the Liberal party.

When examining the decline of the Liberal party in western Canada, one can see two forces at work. First, and most obviously, Trudeau himself, who, like many other Great Men (the parallel here with Lloyd George is interesting), never saw his leadership in terms of building a team or a party. He had a vision of the country and its structure—how it should work. He appears to have had little sense of the party of which he was the leader; he saw it only as a vehicle for accomplishing what he wanted. This is a classic recipe for *après moi, le déluge*, which is what the September 1984 election was all about. And the large number of Liberal senators—longtime veterans as well as recent appointments—reminds us that Lloyd George's lasting contribution to British public life was his creation of an extraordinary number of Liberal peers.

But the blame for the decline of the Liberal party as a force in regional politics cannot be placed entirely at Trudeau's feet. Provincial Liberalism, particularly in western Canada, though by no means only there, responded to the social radicalism of the Co-operative Commonwealth Federation/New Democratic Party by becoming another right-wing party. The result was that Liberalism simply disappeared as an electoral force. Its identity problem was profound and proved to be fatal. There are some signs that this pattern is being repeated on the national scene with the election of John Turner, a corporate lawyer, as leader of the party. Yet Turner is not the first Liberal leader to be a conservative, and so this is hardly an adequate explanation for the decline in Liberal fortunes.

One must look to Quebec itself to see the second large factor in the Liberals' decline. Quebec nationalism is not a passing phenomenon. Yet it will express itself in different ways in different generations. Until now, Quebec voters have elected provincial governments committed to protecting and advancing Quebec's particular interests, and at the same time have sent federalist Liberals to Ottawa in virtually every seat. This situation produced the ironic result that the same voters endorsed René Levesque and Pierre Trudeau and assured them both of majorities. Yet this is not a real inconsistency because both men—in very different ways—were in politics to protect and advance the French fact.

If another political party could convince Quebec voters that another political vehicle could take them to the same destination, the reason for automatically voting Liberal in federal elections would no longer exist. And this is what happened in the election of September 1984. The major reason for the Liberal party's existence—its unique ability to act as a bridge between English and French Canada—has disappeared. The implications of this may be revolutionary, but how revolutionary will depend, of course, on many factors.

The massive victory of John Diefenbaker and the Conservative party in 1958 had the potential to change Canada's political culture. Yet all he really accomplished was the transformation of Canadian political cartooning. As leader of the Conservative landslide victory in 1984, Brian Mulroney has the opportunity to remake the Conservatives as a national party, but the opportunity will depend upon his success in making Quebec as much at home with him and his party as the province has been with the Liberals in the past.

Since about 1920 Canada has had what academics call a "three-party system in transition." Perhaps it is time to stop talking so glibly about transition. The existence of a three-party system has had both great advantages and disadvantages for progressive forces in Canada. Major improvements in health and social security systems would not have taken place without the presence of a democratic left party on the political spectrum.

Yet Canada stands virtually alone among the industrial democracies in having a democratic left party that has a link and connection to the labor movement but has not formed a government and is not yet a clear alternative government. Formed in the wake of the mammoth Conservative victory in 1958, the New Democratic Party was intended to be the rallying point for a progressive coalition. That has yet to happen east of Manitoba, and the New Democratic Party is not yet a majoritarian political force at the national level. That statement could not be made of the Australian Labour party, or the Swedish Social Democrats, or the Spanish

Socialists, or even, in its own unique way, the American Democratic party.

Despite the presence of an established left party accepted as legitimate by voters and with an important influence on the policies of national governments, Canada's expenditures on social security are relatively low when compared to those of other Organization for Economic Cooperation and Development countries, and the labor movement has had profound difficulty in gaining access to the power structures in Canadian society. Peace, order, and good government make for a deferential, conservative political culture. Effervescent, democratic, raucous voices have enormous difficulty being heard, let alone having influence, in Canadian public life, unless filtered through the two parties that see themselves as "Born to Govern."

What, then, of the future of this "system in transition"? American political culture has been deeply affected by Ronald Reagan's two victories. The American Democratic party, despite its almost majoritarian electoral support in Congress, will have to fashion a new coalition if it is to regain the presidency in 1988 and after. Canada's political life has been deeply affected by its own counter-revolution, and the once mighty Liberal party has been reduced to fighting with the New Democratic Party for their quarter or fifth of the popular vote. The election in 1984 saw the Liberals slip to third-party status in English Canada, and a party that is third has to give people an even better reason to vote for it than for a party that is first or second.

I have no crystal ball, but there are some political realities that will persist. In every industrialized democracy in the Western world, the democratic left movement has both a political and an industrial arm. The Liberal party, however, has always avoided any connection or tie with the labor movement and its leadership. A Liberal party convention is very much a middle-class affair, far more so than even Democratic conventions in the United States. There are, as yet, no real signs that the Liberal party wants to change its basic structure in any way or to become more than a party of the center.

Whether the massive Conservative majority in the 1984 election will lead to a decline of the Liberals and a resultant gain for the New Democrats comes down to the voters' perception of the relevance of the two parties. The 1985 Ontario election would seem to indicate that the Liberals, forming a government, albeit a minority one, for the first time in the province in forty-two years, are still taken seriously as an alternative government to the Conservatives in central Canada.

The Conservatives themselves have choices. They can continue to occupy only the right side of the spectrum and hope to make a special regional appeal to Quebec that will return them a certain amount of seats. Or they can go the much smarter route, which is to move into the center and gradually displace the Liberals as the pragmatic centrists of Canadian politics. Both scenarios point to the need for a realignment.

F. R. Scott, a founder of the Co-operative Commonwealth Federation, a poet, and a constitutional lawyer, was one of Canada's great political thinkers and activists. He once wrote of Mackenzie King, the quintessentially Liberal prime minister:

> He blunted us.
>
> We had no shape
> Because he never took sides,
> And no sides
> Because he never allowed them to take shape . . .
>
> Truly he will be remembered
> Wherever men honour ingenuity,
> Ambiguity, inactivity, and political longevity.
>
> Let us raise up a temple,
> To the cult of mediocrity,
> Do nothing by halves
> Which can be done by quarters.

As the leader of the third party in Canada's most populous and most industrial province (and a province that, until 1985, saw one right-centrist party control government for forty-two years), I can readily share Scott's scorn for the comfortable spread of the marshmallow middle, but that frustration has yet to produce a national, progressive, left-of-center government in Ottawa. Nor have the New Democrats done so in Ontario, Canada's largest province, or in any of the provinces east of Manitoba.

A three-party system has made breakthroughs in politics that clearly distinguish Canada from the United States, but for much of the country this system is still innovative, not yet fully embraced or understood. Thus the identity of exactly who lies beyond Tweedledum and Tweedledee can be seen only in shadow and outline. Bringing that figure out of the shadows makes for exciting politics.

Monique Bégin

Medicare—Available to All Canadians

C anada is the Sweden of the Americas. This provocative statement clearly locates Canada for the American public, who tend to take that country for granted as a quiet extension of themselves.

The image of Sweden is, of course, the image par excellence of the welfare state. And although Canada's marginal tax rate is 50 percent—far from the Swedish 80 percent—Canadian residents enjoy a "safety net" of social programs, including a universal and free health system unmatched in the Americas. This fact is, in itself, quite surprising when one considers that origins and developments are so similar in Canada and the United States, two pluralistic democracies whose socioeconomic organizations are almost identical. The United States is advanced in most, if not all, domains of activity, but it lags behind most Western countries when it comes to its social security system, including its health-care delivery system.

This chapter will explore the Canadian scene in relation to one program in particular, the so-called medicare program: how it came into being, and how it survived the recession and continues to grow. We shall then try to understand why Americans do not enjoy such a universal health plan and do not seem even close to having one of their own. In my exploration, I hope I shall not fall into the trap of being ideological. The health status of a given population is what really counts, and that includes, to my way of thinking, the availability and the accessibility of good health and good health care for all segments of a society.

American audiences, when told of Canada's universal health insurance plan, usually react by saying: "Oh, you mean socialized medicine!" And if they know anything about the health sector, they may add: "Great Britain!" Such a reaction offers some indication of a first difference between Canada and the United States, the difference in their political cultures.

For the moment, however, my point is that whatever the system, private, public, or mixed, that is responsible for health-care services, what matters from a public policy point of view is twofold: Who receives the services (is the system really accessible *to all*)? and at what cost (to both the individual and the society)? In other words, is the system equitable and is it efficient?

Canadians generally refer to their free, universal health care as medicare, in French, *l'assurance-santé*. The official name of the Canadian plan comes from the two pieces of legislation establishing it, the Hospital Insurance and Diagnostic Services Act (1957) and the Medical Care Insurance Act (1966). Medicare, which does not mean what it does in the United States, was introduced in Canada in these two stages. In-patient services and, in some provinces, out-patient services became available twenty-eight years ago, and physicians' services at office visits and in hospitals became free nineteen years ago. When I say "free," I mean that the bulk of the health-care system is prepaid and financed through general taxation at both the federal and provincial levels. (Three provinces have added a small premium to general taxation that is imposed on every single or family taxpayer.) When patients go to see a physician or to the hospital, they have nothing to pay. The only health-care services not covered by medicare are dental care, optometrists' services, and drugs, unless these services are provided in a hospital. And, in some provinces, certain categories of citizens, such as children, seniors, and welfare recipients, obtain even these services free of charge. The only charges made to patients are incidentals such as television and telephone rentals and differentials for private or semi-private accommodation, unless privacy is deemed medically necessary.

Some European countries have paralleled their public health system with a private network of clinics and specialists, and in that sense have a private sector more or less undermining their public system. That a double standard exists in such situations is even at times a valid accusation. France and Great Britain are cases in point. Yet it is fair to say that through the ever-increasing need for expensive, high-technology equipment, the public hospital networks of these two countries now enjoy a predominant influence because of massive public investment. (The situation, however, has greatly changed in Great Britain because of the budget cuts of Prime Minister Margaret Thatcher.)

In Canada, after medical studies are completed and professional licenses obtained, young doctors have a number of options; for example, they can open private practices, work on salary in cooperative clinics or government services, or join in partnership with colleagues. There are no administrative districts to which the doctor is assigned. Reciprocally, patients choose their own general practitioners or specialists. For each medical act performed, the general practitioner or the specialist bills the health plan of the province according to a fee schedule, which is negotiated every year or every second year by the provincial government and the medical association of that province. Hospital ownership has not changed; hospitals still belong, at least on paper, to religious orders, corporations (public, semipublic, and even private), or governments; but, in practice, they are "provincial creatures" in that their operating budgets and their capital funding proceed from provincial treasuries. A few hospitals are under federal jurisdiction.

Such an overview leads directly to the Canadian Constitution and the question of jurisdiction. Canada, a federation of ten provinces and two territories, has a federal government and ten provincial governments functioning within a parliamentary system of

British origin. The taxation basis of the federal government corresponds *grosso modo* to one-third of the taxation field, the provinces occupying the remaining two-thirds. The British North America Act (1867) defines the distribution of jurisdictions. Health is under provincial jurisdiction; but, as in other fields of activity, a federal presence has developed over the years, usually through generous financial grants to assist the provinces in the fields of hospital construction, training of health professionals, public health research, public health programs, and programs for the control of specific diseases. As a consequence of provincial jurisdiction, national policies are difficult to develop and implement in such a complex and politically sensitive environment. But whenever "cooperative federalism" works, the results are usually excellent for Canadians in terms of a better quality of life. Medicare is no exception.

Twenty-five years ago, the Canadian health-care scene was much the same as it is now in the United States. People protected themselves against the risks of illness either by means of a private insurance plan or through one linked to their employment. Most families and individuals were left to their own devices when it came to paying for health services, and the range and the quality of available services depended more or less on what people could afford to pay. Low-income households had to resort to various types of "charity" medicine and to government assistance. "Free wards" in hospitals, public clinics, sanatoria, and charitable hostels ministered to the health needs of the indigent.

In some cases, the health services given low-income patients were quite acceptable. Indeed, in teaching hospitals, some physicians boasted that the poor—particularly if they had "interesting" illnesses—actually enjoyed treatment superior to that received by regular paying patients. The health care available to most poor Canadians, however, was minimal. Health care was a market commodity. The poor, whether they attended a physician's office, the charity ward of a hospital, or an outpatient clinic, received their health services as a handout, with all the stigma that this entails in our society. I remember such an experience myself in the fifties and sixties. My father, though an engineer, was not wealthy, for there were nine in the family. He died of cancer in a charity ward of a Montreal hospital after three years of hospitalization. My mother died shortly after, and I, the eldest, remember being unable to pay the medical bills.

For all but the affluent, a serious or chronic illness, especially one that required a lengthy stay in the hospital, became a passport to poverty. Not only did mounting medical bills eat up families' savings, but work lost because of illness or disability reduced earning capacity and made matters worse. The expense of consulting a doctor for checkups and for diagnosis of health problems also prevented many middle-income Canadians from seeking medical care, with the result that treatment was often sought only in the later, more dangerous stages of an illness. As in the United States today, numbers of personal bankruptcies due to medical bills and payments were registered every year.

To ease the burden of everyday health-care expenses and to protect themselves from the financial catastrophe of major illness, many people turned to private health insurance. A bewildering variety of medical and hospital insurance schemes developed after World War II. Some private sector plans were run by hospitals and by physicians, others by commercial insurance companies. This hodge-podge of health insurance schemes left much to be desired. A major failing was their incomplete coverage of the population. In the late fifties, less than 40 percent of the population had any form of hospital insurance protection. In 1961, only 59 percent of all Canadians had some form of medical insurance, which was usually purchased from private carriers, and more than one-third of the entire population had no insurance whatsoever to help pay medical bills.

Private health insurance operated much like automobile insurance. When patients filed claims, they had to pay an initial fixed amount (the deductible) out of their own pockets before the insurance plan took over the expenses. If the patient made too many claims because of frequent illness, the premium rates would rise. Worse still, those who needed health insurance the most—the poor, the elderly, the chronically ill—were least likely to qualify for insurance coverage. The elderly and people with a record of serious or recurring illness were considered poor insurance risks. They either were charged exorbitant premiums, which few could afford, or were refused membership by private insurance plans. Not only were health insurance schemes uneven in coverage, cost, and quality, but their sheer numbers defied logic. When the province of Ontario joined medicare, it counted more than two hundred separate insurers. Surveyed from a national perspective, health insurance was like a tattered quilt, thin in places and filled with holes, rather than the thick and uniform blanket of protection needed to cover all Canadians.

Such was the background, and of course, medicare did not come into being magically or overnight. Although this description of the situation can well apply to the United States today, Canadian historical roots and developments differed enough from the American scene to constitute a key factor in a national public health plan.

The Great Depression led to the creation, in 1933, in western Canada, of a socialist party: the Co-operative Commonwealth Federation, since 1961 the New Democratic Party. On the federal scene, the New Democratic Party enjoys a more or less constant 18 percent of the votes, and holds, at the moment, 30 seats out of the 282 in the House of Commons. In August 1943, the Co-operative Commonwealth Federation became the official opposition in Ontario, and in June 1944, formed the government in Saskatchewan. It now forms the government in the province of Manitoba under Premier Howard Pawley. The New Democratic Party, more or less in the tradition of the British Labour party, was a strong advocate of social security measures, regularly feeding public opinion with possible social reforms and nurturing the hopes for a complete social security program that included national health insurance.

World War II led to the thinking in many quarters that the war efforts and sacrifices could be justified only if social and economic reforms were brought in as priorities for government action. This view was shared by the Liberal prime minister, Mackenzie King, and was taken into account in postwar policy making. A first attempt toward a national health plan was presented to the provinces in August 1945, following a formal pledge during that spring's election campaign. The conference that considered this proposal reached a deadlock on the tax provisions and, despite years of preparation, collapsed. But at least a new national policy proposal for health insurance had been brought into public focus, with federal and provincial government input as well as input from the medical profession—enough participation so that the proposal could never be dismissed in the future.

It was only in 1955, ten years later, that federal-provincial negotiations reopened, leading to the first stage of a national medicare, with a plan for the public coverage of hospital care as a first step. It took more than ten years before the legislation extending public coverage to medical services at the hospital and in physicians' offices was enacted on July 1, 1968. The legislation fulfilled a fifty-year commitment to health insurance by the ruling Liberal party. This government achievement would never have been possible without the challenge and the support of T. C. Douglas and Stanley Knowles of the New Democrats. The final vote in the House of Commons is worthy of mention, for it forced, so to speak, a positive vote from the Progressive Conservative party, which was pushed by the generally strong support of the public. When the final vote was recorded on December 8, 1966, 177 members of Parliament voted in favor of the legislation and 2 voted against it. (When the same bill had passed its second reading on October 25, and only after a very acrimonious debate, there had been 21 votes against it.)

Two major events played a critical role in achieving the second phase of medicare at that time: the public health plan introduced in two stages by the Co-operative Commonwealth Federation's provincial government of T. C. Douglas in Saskatchewan in 1946 and in 1961, and the Royal Commission on Health Services headed by Mr. Justice Emmett Hall, which recommended in 1964 that medical-care insurance be introduced. The personal leadership of these two great Canadians must be underlined in a special way, for Canadians owe them a great debt in the long battle toward the establishment of one of the best health plans in existence, a plan known, admired, and respected all over the world.

The main actors in this long awaited reform consisted of the federal government and the ten provincial governments, the political parties (both caucus and membership), the public, and the health professions. As for the media, it was always there, but I would suggest that it became a strong player only in the last five years—during the debate about extra-billing, the one serious crisis medicare has gone through since its inception. Other socio-economic groups, business lobbies in particular, played secondary roles as conservative forces, except for the private insurance industry, which reached a peak in its opposition to medicare when the province of Ontario debated a health plan of its own in the early fifties. Academics were involved only marginally, except for individual health economists who, like the media, played a positive key role in the recent medicare crisis.

It would be misleading not to spend some time now on one main actor in this social drama—the medical profession. In pre-medicare days, physicians practiced in the same way as they do now, but for those settling in a small, rural, or isolated community there was severe hardship, because in such areas there were many people who could not afford to pay their medical bills. I was often told by doctors that, no matter where they practiced, they could, as a rule, never collect more than 60 to 75 percent of the value of their bills. The Great Depression had left local governments almost bankrupt, and the national as well as the provincial medical associations were very conscious of this serious problem. In the thirties, the Canadian Medical Association pressed the federal government for a sharing program to meet part of the costs of hospital and medical care. The only response came in a minimal form in a few of the provinces, Manitoba and Alberta, and especially Saskatchewan and British Columbia. There were strong feelings in the association during the thirties that the health status of the population was at stake (official statistics using the critical indicator of infant mortality rates in 1937 ranked Canada in the seventeenth place among developed countries); that no preventive medicine could be practiced; and that physicians were not adequately paid. In 1934, the association released a report concluding that "government health insurance was necessary and, in view of the obvious interest of the public in it, probably inevitable."

That cooperative mood passed the test of Saskatchewan's first step toward medicare—its Hospital Services Plan of 1946. But when the second test came in 1961 to the same province—still innovative under the leadership of T. C. Douglas—the relationship between the medical profession and the provincial government had seriously deteriorated. A very bitter and tragic strike by physicians and specialists began on July 1, 1962, not ending until July 23. And the compromises reached by the Saskatchewan government in the settlement of the dispute shaped forever the medicare system that Canadians now enjoy from coast to coast. The development of medicare in Canada went through another dramatic moment in the province of Quebec when the specialists, after several work slowdowns, went on strike on October 1, 1970, prior to the passage of the legislation that established medical-care insurance in that province. Special legislation passed on October 15, 1970, forced the specialists back to work.

As in the case of the Saskatchewan strike, the themes returned to by the medical profession in Quebec were that "socialized-state" medicine threatened the liberty and freedom of physicians; threatened the quality of care; threatened the "rights of the patient" (whatever the phrase means); and threatened massive emigration of physicians and specialists to the United States. It is interesting that years later, when medicare had to go through the recession and meet its first real crisis in the spread of extra-billing from 1979 until 1984, the very same language and themes were used by the medical profession in fighting the federal government. What was at stake, in fact, in most of the cases was the physicians' fears that their income would decline. In both situations, as in physicians' strikes generally, the public reacted most ambivalently—at first they were supportive of the government, but then became increasingly fearful that they might lose the services of their own physician.

Medicare had, among many positive results, one especially happy consequence for the medical profession. It guaranteed physicians an annual income without any particular administrative burdens and with no further need to resort to collecting agencies. As a consequence, physicians settled more and more into small, isolated communities, no longer afraid of unpaid bills due to local poverty. All this is not to say that the situation is perfect: there are still problems in attracting physicians to the two territories, the

Indian reserves, and, generally, the northern parts of the provinces. But the point can be easily made that medicare is good for physicians and good for hospitals. According to the official statistics released yearly by Revenue Canada, for last year, as well as for every preceding year, physicians remain the highest paid group in Canada.

Medicare has also proven to be very good for the Canadian public. The key health indicators all showed a clear trend toward a healthier population following the implementation of medicare.

In terms of administrative costs and efficiency, medicare has been a sound proposition. The Canadian public health-care system has an annual cost of approximately twenty billion dollars. Another ten billion represents the private sector of health, for example, dental services, pharmaceutical industry, optometrist services, and nursing homes. In the past decade, according to rankings by country supplied by the Organization for Economic Cooperation and Development, Canada is usually in the middle range of health expenditures. A chart including both public and private health spending would indicate that Canada was slightly ahead of the United States in terms of costs from 1960 to 1965, but was then bypassed in the late sixties by the United States and its widening gap of expenditures; health-care costs remained constant or showed only moderate increases in the eighties. During the seventies, Canadian health-care costs as a percentage of the Gross National Product were virtually stable at about 7 percent. At the same time, the American percentages rose considerably until 1982, when the United States spent 10.5 percent of its Gross National Product on health care compared to a Canadian figure of 8.3 percent.

What program does not have problems? The recent recession made all social programs vulnerable to cuts, but despite the prevailing neoconservative economic philosophy and strong pressures from other countries and from international forums like the Organization for Economic Cooperation and Development, Canada maintained and even improved her social security net, including medicare, from 1978 until 1984.

Medicare came under attack as early as February 1979, when questions were raised in both the Ontario legislature and the federal House of Commons as to the new and growing practice of extra-billing by physicians and user fees by hospitals. There then began what was to become one of the most difficult and important issues of the federal government until the time of the election of September 1984. (It should be remembered that there never was, before 1979, more than 10 percent of physicians who extra-billed their patients.)

To summarize the medicare crisis over extra-billing would require a written history of recent events and extensive research to establish all the facts. Such tasks are yet to be undertaken. I shall offer, therefore, my own version based on my recollection of events in which I was directly involved.

As the recession hit Canada, Canadians witnessed the rise of two over-charge practices, one by physicians and one by provincial governments through hospitals, both practices made possible by a serious weakness in the otherwise sound legislation passed by the federal government under the Established Programs Financing Act (1977). I was not a member of the Cabinet at the time of the creation of this legislation—I was sworn in as Minister of National Revenue on September 15, 1976—and I do not know how extensive and serious the discussions were of the shortcomings in the legislation. Some provincial health ministers did confirm to me that they had more than once made the point that loopholes in the act would drive physicians to extra-bill their patients.

After much public debate, federal-provincial discussions, meetings with the health professions, a special inquiry and recommendations by Mr. Justice Emmett Hall (the same man who in 1964 had recommended establishing a national medical-care insurance program and who presented a second report to me in September 1980), and a report from a parliamentary committee, "Fiscal Federalism in Canada: Report of the Parliamentary Task Force on Federal-Provincial Fiscal Arrangements" (August 1981), it became evident that legislative action was the only route left to correct the situation. After extensive and crucial studies of the jurisdictional issue, the new Canada Health Act (1984) was tabled in the House of Commons on December 12, 1983, and passed unanimously by all three political parties on April 9, 1984.

In this very heated period, the groups involved were the same as in 1956 and in 1967, but the individuals were not, nor were the times. At first glance, the battle seemed impossible to win. The public was not aware of the problem; the medical profession opposed any government action; the provinces forcefully opposed the federal government, some arguing that there was no problem, others that they could do nothing about the situation. And, of course, the general mood of the country was to believe that people abused the system and that relatively small user charges were perfect deterrents against such abuses. In fact, patients have little say over use of most health services. Admissions to hospitals are controlled by physicians. Self-admission is simply not possible. Over 70 percent of total health-care costs are made up of hospital inpatient care, and physicians, not patients, made the decisions regarding the use of these services.

Designing a strategy to meet such circumstances was quite an intellectual challenge. I think it fair to say that it was the public support, quite solid after a long and quiet awakening, that won the battle. It is also realistic to note that the federal bureaucracy (at the top echelons, not in middle management), the Cabinet, and the caucus (the latter under siege from lobbies of physicians in the members' individual constituencies) were—to state the case mildly—far from convinced that there was any problem at all. The media kept the issue alive over several months, even years, digging up evidence of restricted access, comparing the Canadian situation to that of other countries, reporting faithfully any new attempt by provinces, the Canadian Medical Association, or provincial medical associations to escalate the issue. Small groups of citizens and physicians here and there in the country organized themselves as early as the fall of 1979, some by themselves, others around the Canadian Labour Congress or the New Democratic Party, later with the Liberals, trying their best to alert the public and the governments to the dangers of erosion of medicare. Two quasi-commissions of inquiry served as platforms for all these groups to prepare and present briefs and recommendations. But the means at their disposal were very modest compared to the money the Canadian Medical Association put into the dispute. There were, however, the voices of Mr. Justice Emmett Hall and of health economists that gave credibility, at least the beginning of credibility, to those who had assessed the situation as very grave and feared the introduction into Canada of the kind of double-standard medicine that had developed, for example, in Australia under the Conservative government.

Among the various aspects of the issue was, as a key constraint, the critical problem of assessing what powers, if any, the federal government had in relation to the provinces (and, indirectly, to the physicians) to control the practice of extra-billing. Would the existing legislation stand in courts as forbidding such additional charges? Was the issue in any way federal? Was the jurisprudence on the interpretation of the federal "spending power" going to en-tertain charges of breaches of the legislation? The next practical, key constraint was that the existing legislation had only one pen-alty in cases of breaches of its conditions: the complete withdrawal of the monthly cash payment by the federal government to a prov-ince found guilty. Such an eventuality would have justified prov-inces, politically speaking, in closing emergency clinics and hospi-tal wards, which would lead to possibly tragic occurrences. Such situations would have turned off the public support or, still worse, given arguments for physicians to strike—events to be avoided at all costs, to say the least.

Technical work was undertaken at my request by the Depart-ment of National Health and Welfare to draft legislation. Such leg-islation had to clarify the five basic conditions to be met by the provinces in order to qualify for the federal cash contributions de-termined in the Established Programs Financing Act. The legisla-tion also had to link the breach of these conditions to a practical and workable set of penalties, both efficient and fair, which would have teeth but would not provoke a shutdown of insured health services. At the same time, outside expertise and advice were sought on the constitutional aspect of the question. A quiet but significant mobilization of public opinion was initiated and kept alive during the last two years of this crisis. I felt very strongly that the use of expensive advertising by the federal government would be counterproductive. In any event, the advertising was not neces-sary. The public, as I knew, was very fond of medicare. The problem was that the number of people affected by extra-billing and user fees was not large enough to generate a public outcry of anger and frustration. The crisis was of the nature of erosion—it would be difficult to make the public aware of its seriousness until it was too late and the institution of medicare had collapsed.

The difficulties of a public discussion were compounded by groups of supporters of medicare, especially the health professionals *other* than physicians, who seized the opportunity to re-open a general comprehensive debate on every possible reform to be brought to the health-care delivery system—most of which reforms were provincial in jurisdiction and called for increased provincial funding. Nurses, for example, were vocal and articulate in their demands, and they were, in my opinion, absolutely right in their points. But there was no way that the *rapport de forces,* everything taken into account, would allow me in the name of the federal government to reopen the question of health-service delivery and fight on a wide front. The demand had to be on strict and clear points: no extra-charges would be permitted in order to respect the letter and the spirit of the Established Programs Financing Act.

By June 1983, it was evident from the polls that, in each of the ten provinces, the public was supportive of the federal stand on medicare in the order of 75 to 80 percent. Only then and with favorable legal advice was the battle to be undertaken as its own by the federal government. Events began to develop in a systematic way toward the unanimous passage in the House of Commons of the new Canada Health Act in early April 1984.

What was essentially at stake in this major public debate in Canada? I think it fair to state that the question, for both the provincial treasuries and physicians or, more accurately, organized medicine, was one of money, disguised, of course, behind every possible argument. No one could state the case loudly, yet it was—I am tempted to state "only"—a question of money. In a report, "Medicare; The Public Good and Private Practice," from the National Council of Welfare in May 1982, the matter was clearly stated:

> The fact that user fees for health care are ineffective, harmful
> and unpopular with the public has not made them the dinosaur

policy they deserve to be. To the contrary, there is mounting pressure from two powerful sources—the medical profession and several provincial governments—to expand the use of direct patient charges.

The Canadian Medical Association strongly supports extra-billing, opposes any proposal to ban the practice, and has criticized Quebec's refusal to reimburse patients whose doctors charge more than the approved fee schedule. By threatening either to engage in or increase extra-billing, several provincial medical associations (notably those in Ontario, British Columbia and Alberta) have used the practice as a bargaining tool in their negotiations with provincial governments over medicare fees.

The latest instance is the Alberta Medical Association, which called on its members to extra-bill their patients because the provincial government gave a 21 percent fee increase for 1982 instead of the 30.5 percent demanded by the doctors.

My analysis of the recent and only real crisis medicare went through is necessarily incomplete and biased. Nuances are missing and, in a way, much more should be stated. But the purpose of this essay is to describe a major Canadian institution without hiding the problems it had to resolve, and then to go on with a view to understanding the structural political differences between Canada and the United States. As I stated at the opening of these reflections, I see significant differences between the two countries on account of differing political culture and political institutions.

Unlike the United States, Canada has never feared "socialistic" measures to the point of panic. On one level, the political socialist tradition of the Co-operative Commonwealth Federation/New Democratic Party has been rooted in Canada since the Great Depression, and has never been viewed as an import from Europe. Moreover, this tradition, which began in western Canada, developed in rural areas as well as in cities, and it became enough of the mainstream to form several provincial governments. The links with Great Britain and with France, maintained by the two "founding nations," kept European initiatives under scrutiny and discussion. In contrast, the political socialist tradition of a state like Wisconsin, a very local socialist tradition, directly expressed through European—mainly German—immigrants, never really developed a national basis in the United States. That tradition remained very much a Milwaukee phenomenon for more than half a century. In the United States, the need for socioeconomic reforms, so deeply felt after the Great Depression, was expressed in the New Deal by mainstream American politicians, yet no permanent political structure pushed for socioeconomic reforms on a systematic basis.

Even if Canadians and Americans both have capitalist economies with related value systems and political rhetoric, the Canadian economy has remained mixed, with active "interference" by government—for example, ownership, nationalization, and new ventures—throughout the history of the Canadian federation. The mixed economy stems basically from the Canadian need for self-assertion against a powerful neighbor, since Canada has a very small population spread along the southern border of a vast, rich, and empty land. For example, the need to avoid cultural colonization led to the creation, in 1932, of what is now the Canadian Broadcasting Corporation, and cultural public policy making remained an active role of the federal government throughout recent decades, culminating in the new Broadcasting Act of 1968 and the Canadian ownership and Canadian content regulations of the Canadian Radio and Television Commission of the early seventies. And the quest for a distinct national identity remains a constant preoccupation of the commission's public policies. Examples of direct government initiatives can be found in almost every field of human endeavor. Such initiatives exist to keep the country together, counteracting the natural centripetal tendencies of the Canadian nation as a very fragmented society. Canada never was the American "melting pot." It managed to evolve a political culture based on multiple tensions and accommodations among internal subgroups: a culture that is bilingual within a multicultural framework; pluralistic and pluri-religious, yet with a sense of collective solidarity; extremely decentralized with strong provincial governments and marked regional differences, yet a federation; a highly participatory process, yet a stable democracy.

Such reflections take us back to the idea Canadians have of their government. The public view of the role of the federal government—and this is true to a lesser degree of the public's perception of the provincial governments—whatever the party in office, is quite different from the traditional American attitudes toward federal and state governments. And though not a specialist, I would submit that the difference of perception and attitude is not only sociological and cultural, but also one rooted in the legal institutions of the two countries. For example, the overriding principle in the Constitution of the United States is the protection of individual rights through the limitation of governmental power. When Canada became a federation in 1867, powers were allocated between the two levels of government by the British North America Act but no individual rights were entrenched. This dimension came only with the patriation of the Canadian Constitution and the Constitution Act of 1982. (Canadians have had a Bill of Rights since 1960, but it applied only to federal laws; the Bill always received a very restrictive interpretation, and never saw the guarantees of individual rights entrenched.) Americans grew as a nation with their Constitution shaping their lives and their political traditions; the Constitution framed their political institutions, and it was invested in time with a powerful symbolic as well as legal significance. The American Constitution clearly affected the mental images and beliefs the American public held in regard to their government. That historical process did not take place in Canada.

For Canadians, the government is very much a tool of action and a resource to be used in times of need or in situations of crisis—notwithstanding the usual and normal criticisms and sarcasms about "too much red tape" and "too high taxes." In the area of health care, one can state that in the Canadian political culture, a national consensus has been reached that health, like education, is not and should not be a market commodity. Health is seen as a collective or public good.

The final point I wish to make touches another reason why Americans will not easily, if ever, see a universal, free health system adopted in the United States. This reason stems from a fundamental difference not in the political culture, but in the political institutions of the two countries: the Canadian parliamentary system and the American presidential system. This observation is offered as a hypothesis still requiring research before eventual validation. Viewed as a vehicle for political action—including all stages of the decision-making process as well as the legislative process—the parliamentary system is a highly integrated mechanism. It poses few disruptions in carrying through complex and controversial policies. Once adopted by a political party for its official platform during a general election, a collective project such as a universal medicare plan would then be promoted by the elected members of Parliament in their weekly caucus meetings with the Cabinet. The prime minister and Cabinet, after the usual study stages by committees of Cabinet, would authorize the bill to be tabled in the House of Commons directly by the minister or ministers responsible. The bill would receive a party vote at every stage of its three readings in the House of Commons. I believe that in the United States the path to action would be much more fluid, less in the open, and far more vulnerable to compromises and accommodations to personal interests in the case of the Congress and the Senate. To this should be added the different power of lobby groups within the two systems.

In lieu of conclusion, I would like to offer a final comment. This chapter is both a plea for a health system accessible and equitable for all, and an effort to explain Canada and Canadians to the United States. It is amazing to see how much the two countries look alike. Yet basic, important dimensions distinguish them. I often wonder if the sheer numbers, the very fact that the United States has a population ten times larger than Canada, do not change the nature of the political process of both countries. But this reflection is for another time!

Walter Stewart

The Seven Myths of Journalism

A few years ago, the dean of Arts at the University of Saskatchewan in Regina asked the head of the Department of English if he would introduce a course in journalism in his department. The English professor replied, "Not until they teach streetwalking in Home Economics."

There is now a course in journalism at the University of Saskatchewan, but I don't know what they're up to over in Home Economics. What this incident shows is that journalism, like streetwalking, is in popular demand, even if sometimes in low repute.

Journalists like to think that theirs is one of the higher callings; and, to this end, we have succeeded in concocting a series of myths about our craft to enhance it. It is my purpose to explore these myths, which are seven in number. In each case, there is some substance behind it, but, in each case, the general weight of evidence goes counter to it. Because I am a Canadian, I shall try to set out differences—where they exist—that affect the operation of the myths in Canada and in the United States.

I. The Myth of Objectivity

The myth of objectivity embodies a view—more widely held within journalistic circles than among the general public—that journalists can be counted upon to view people and events around them with scientific detachment.

Harrison Salisbury summed this view up in the title of his book about the *New York Times,* which he called *Without Fear or Favor.* Much of the book details how fear or favor—sometimes both—guided the fortunes and the reporting of a newspaper widely (and correctly) held to be one of the finest in the world. For example, Salisbury cites a study by Walter Lippmann and Charles Merz in 1920 which found that on ninety-one occasions between November 1917 and November 1919, the *Times* had reported that the Bolshevik regime in Russia had fallen or was about to fall. "Fourteen times the collapse of the Bolsheviks was said to be in progress, four times Lenin and Trotsky were reported as preparing to flee, three times they had already fled, twice Lenin was reported to be retiring, once he had been killed and three times he had been thrown into prison." There was no substantive evidence behind any of these reports; they represented the wishful thinking of the correspondents, editors, and readers of the *New York Times.*

The release of the Pentagon Papers, the central event around which Salisbury's book is woven, was brought about by a group of men who had in mind the exposure, denunciation, and punishment of the architects of United States involvement in Vietnam. Salisbury quotes Neil Sheehan, the reporter who got the Pentagon Papers from Daniel Ellsberg, as saying that their publication "would ruin the Bundys (and) the McNamaras" and that "the cleansing of the nation's conscience and the future conduct of the most powerful country in the world . . . demand a national inquiry into the war crimes question."

Right on, I say, but no one would contend that what Sheehan had in mind was a cool, dispassionate, objective review of the origins of Vietnam. What he wanted brought before the public gaze was all the damaging material that had been hidden so long from view—not as a matter of curiosity, but as a corrective. The publication of the Pentagon Papers was a milestone in United States journalism; but it was not, and was not intended to be, "objective" journalism.

I do not believe such a thing as objective journalism exists, or that it would be of much use if it did. Take political journalism. I cannot imagine a journalist of intelligence, sent to cover politics in Washington for four years, who could refrain from forming his own conclusions about the political process, and reflecting those conclusions in his work, one way or another. If you want to know what goes on in a harem, don't ask a eunuch. He may have a grasp of the mechanics, but he doesn't have the flavor of the proceedings.

If journalism were objective, a reporter from Iowa and a reporter from Cairo would compile essentially the same report of an OPEC meeting. A journalist from Toronto and another from Mitchell, North Dakota, would come to the same conclusions about the Garrison Diversion scheme. There would be no point in sending a *New York Times* man to Ottawa—any Canadian who had been stationed in Washington for a few years could handle the chore.

If journalism were objective, American readers would not have been told, after Castro came to power in Cuba, that his regime was resented, and that he was in constant danger of being overthrown, while Canadian readers were being told by their journalists that Castro was far more successful, far more popular, far more secure than Batista, the right-wing dictator he overthrew to establish his own left-wing dictatorship. The United States might even have been spared the Bay of Pigs, a debacle brought on by massive miscalculation, aided by the deliberate suppression of information in stories carried by, among others, the *New York Times*.

Science is objective in that the same results will flow from the same experiment in New York, Bangkok, or Leningrad. Journalism has none of that rigorous detachment, and only misleads itself when it uses language that suggests that it has. What we can ask of journalists is that they be on guard against their own bias and that they strive for fairness—quite a different thing from objectivity. What we should insist on for ourselves is that there are enough competitive sources of information available to allow us to see more than one side of public issues.

There is no particular Canadian application to the myth of objectivity; it exists in about the same proportion and produces about the same consequences in Canada and in the United States.

2. *The Myth of Belligerence*

Closely allied to the notion that journalism is objective is the notion that journalists are sturdily independent creatures, beholden to no one. Indeed, the myth goes further and suggests that journalists are often the "real opposition" to government. They are a tough, hard-nosed, quarrelsome group who take pride in their cantankerous approach to life. H. L. Mencken noted: "All successful newspapers are ceaselessly querulous and bellicose. They never defend anyone or anything if they can help it; if the job is forced upon them, they tackle it by denouncing someone or something else."

I am an admirer of H. L. Mencken but I think the real state of affairs was more accurately put by the English poet who wrote:

> No one can bribe or twist
> Thank God, the British journalist;
> But, seeing what unbribed he'll do
> There's never any reason to.

It is true that, in their editorials, newspapers are sometimes quarrelsome and shrill. But who reads editorials, anyway? I note in passing that television commentaries, even television editorials, are almost invariably exercises in mush-mouthing. Readers who object to an editorial simply turn the page. They who object to a television editorial flip the dial, and are lost to the advertiser.

The overwhelming proportion of material in any newspaper, radio or television newscast is supportive—supportive of government, of business, of community organizations, chambers of commerce, service clubs, the United Appeal. Trot out a worthy cause—worthy in the eyes of the worthy—and journalism is on hand, drumsticks at the ready to beat out a tattoo of support.

A small but significant part of journalism consists of criticism, and even that usually takes the form of whining rather than attacking. Despite a general view that all that journalists do is complain, the bulk of any newspaper is divided between straightforward accounts of events ranging from wars to the results of a state lottery, and "soft journalism," that is to say, cute stories, offbeat features, interviews with pop stars, horoscopes, medical advice, comics, recipes, fashion layouts—with the name of the store in bold face—gossip columns, and household hints.

In television, the dominant medium, criticism voiced directly by journalists is almost entirely absent. It appears in public affairs shows like "60 Minutes" and lasts about sixty minutes out of every week. News broadcasts on television have become increasingly part of the entertainment world. If this trend continues, "Three's Company" will soon mean Dan Rather, Roger Mudd, and Barbara Walters. News is read by showbiz hosts, at showbiz salaries, with cheerful chatter between the items, and gimmickry to sell the show.

It was a matter of some significance recently when CBS, breaking new ground in journalism, began to move its camera in closer on Dan Rather during the evening news, to make him a more dominant figure. Van Gordon Sauter, head of CBS News, said, "Give me a show without a star, and I'll give you a failed show." Stars do not criticize or attack; they preen.

In an important, perhaps the most important sector of journalism, bellicosity is not merely muted, it is almost absent. Even in the newspaper, it is the exception, not the rule.

The major function of the media is not belligerent and independent comment, but the conveyance of information on everything from the fact that someone has been doping the Tylenol to the fact that the president of the United States has something on his mind, which is often hard to prove. The politicians who complain about the hostility of the media have learned to play the information system like a zither. Just before the 1982 congressional elections, President Reagan launched a series of fireside chats chockablock with the purest propaganda, and the Democrats immediately piled onto the back of his neck. Journalists held their coats. Journalism provided the platform, the air time, and the news reports, summarizing the exchange of insults. The media served, as it so often does, merely as a conduit for information. This is a proper function for journalism, but it occupies far more of our time and space than criticism or even analysis. If you are the zither on which a tune is played, it is not accurate to pretend that you are independent of the process.

Journalists are tied to their society in ways that range all the way from free passes for baseball writers to background briefings for the wise lads who cover Washington. Newspaper proprietors receive subsidized mail rates and show no inclination to shuck them off. Journalists are accorded special privileges in courtrooms, in legislatures, in city halls and sheriff's offices. All the media are dependent on government cooperation at all levels, on advertising revenue, and on the firms that provide that revenue.

It is one of the pleasant fables of the news business that it is immune to advertising pressure. In thirty years as a journalist, I have never yet come across a newspaper, magazine, or television outlet that did not, one way or another, respond to advertisers. What is rare, what is worthy of note, is when journalism does not bow to such pressure. Directly asserted, the threat to withdraw advertising may backfire, but that seldom occurs. What happens is that a newspaper about to run a story likely to offend a major advertiser will contact him to make certain it has "his side of the story." This is known as "acting responsibly"; it is also known as "saving the account." On magazines, it is common practice to inform an advertiser of any adverse comment appearing in a given issue so that advertisements may be withdrawn or shifted. It is common practice for cigarette advertisers, duly forewarned, to withdraw from any issue of the magazine containing articles that mention the word "cancer." After you have done this a few times, and seen advertising revenues evaporate, it is remarkable how unenthusiastic editors can become about articles dealing with cancer.

The only major news operation I have ever encountered that was free of advertising pressure is the radio network of the Canadian Broadcasting Corporation—for the sound reason that it carries no advertising.

In Canada, history, custom, and necessity have led us to recognize that, with so few people and so much geography, we had to use government agencies as major instruments of national development. Thus it appears normal to Canadians to have a government-owned railway, airline, and broadcasting service. We even have a government-owned oil company. The Canadian Broadcasting Corporation, formed in 1935, is a dominant force in Canadian journalism; and, while its television network tends to ape its American counterparts, its radio network is ad free and produces some excellent journalism. Unfortunately, and perhaps inevitably, in substitution for advertising pressure, the Canadian Broadcasting Corporation from time to time comes under political pressure, as the federal government decides that it is the national will that in times of crisis—and we are always in times of crises—the proper role for the journalist is modest stillness and humility.

What I am arguing is that kicking over traces is not the normal function of journalism. When it happens—and, thank God, it does happen—journalists go into paroxysms of self-congratulation, saluting their own sturdy independence. Much of what they salute does not exist; much of their time and effort is spent dispensing conventional wisdom and supporting the status quo.

In the United States, cockiness in journalism has become part of the television news: the brash interviewer embarrassing the bigwig with the penetrating question. Without being unduly cynical, I may conclude that these encounters have more to do with entertainment than with journalism. Viewers like to see a television personality challenging a politician (unless the politician happens to be the president, in which case, tough questioning is regarded as bad form); but, even at that, the number of occasions on which an interviewer actually penetrates the guard of the interviewee is small. Interviews that are conducted to elicit information—rather than merely to entertain—are usually rambling, complex, and civil. Most questions begin with, "I wonder if you could explain . . . ," rather than with, "Do you expect me to believe. . . ."

In short, belligerence in journalism is blessed, but rare.

3. The Myth of the Tireless Investigator

There was a time when the discriminating public had a view of the press reflected in the words of Richard Sheridan: "The newspapers! Sir, they are the most villanous, licentious, abominable, infernal—not that I ever read them." There are still some who hold this view, but it is offset, more than offset, by a popular vision of the hard-digging, indefatigable journalist as seen on "Lou Grant." Journalists, in particular, know what journalists are like— Dustin Hoffman and Robert Redford in *All the President's Men.* Of course, what was obvious about Woodward and Bernstein, the characters portrayed by Redford and Hoffman, was that they are freaks, oddballs, misfits. Even at the *Washington Post,* they were regarded as abnormal. And so they were.

During the weeks and months that the Watergate scandal was oozing over Washington, there were more than seventeen hundred daily newspapers operating in this country. Of these, three—the *Washington Post,* the *New York Times,* and the *Los Angeles Times*— devoted major resources to the story. Everybody else did pretty much what newspapers do best—they tore the stuff off the wire, rewrote it, and printed it.

Real investigation, original investigation, is not the norm in journalism. It happens, certainly, but it is only a tiny portion of what a handful of journalists do. I happen to think it is the most important portion, but that is another issue entirely; mostly what journalism does consists of writing down what somebody says, and making sense of it.

The clearest example of what I mean is contained in Salisbury's *Without Fear or Favor,* where the author rightly salutes the release of the Pentagon Papers as an act of significance and bravery. The reporter who got the scoop in the first place was Neil Sheehan, one of the nation's best investigators. And what did Sheehan do? Well, the most important thing he did was to borrow a copy of the papers from Daniel Ellsberg, and then he and his wife holed up in the Treadway Inn in Cambridge, Massachusetts, for three days while they ran off a copy on the trusty old Xerox machine. There was more to it than that, of course, but that was the nub of it. The real investigation of the Pentagon Papers was not done by Sheehan or anyone else on the *New York Times,* but by the experts in the administration who had been working on it for years. The journalist's role was to copy the information, read it, analyze it, sort it out, and lay it before the public. This is the task of journalists, nearly all of the time. They are essentially borrowers: they ransack the brains, books, and files of other people who have done the investigating, rewrite it, and put it into print or onto the air. It is worthy work, but it is rarely investigative and mostly passive.

Recently, in both Canada and the United States, we have witnessed the rise of small, earnest, and entirely worthy bodies called Centers for Investigative Journalism. Their purpose is to form a common bond among journalists foolhardy enough to be interested in this aspect of the craft, and to lend aid—mostly moral—to the process. Speakers are brought in to tell young practitioners how to conduct a title search, how to read an annual report, how to interpret statistics. Much sober thought is also expended on the issue of whether there is, in fact, such a thing as investigative journalism. One view holds that all journalism is, or should be, investigative, and it is therefore pretentious and wrong for journalists to stick a capital "I" up there in Investigative to signal their intentions to the world. In fact, however, there are a series of questions any journalist can put to himself to determine if he is, or is not, working on the kind of journalism that deserves a capital "I":

> Did I give my right name at all times?
> Do I want the piece checked by a libel lawyer?
> Does my managing editor want the piece checked by a libel lawyer?
> Have I hidden my notes?
> Did it take me six weeks to complete the assignment?
> Are some of my sources known only to me and my immediate editor?
> Are we negotiating for the movie rights?

If the answers to these questions are No, Yes, Yes, Yes, Yes, Yes, and Yes, then either the piece is investigative or the journalist is making a hell of a fuss over an article on how to raise delphiniums.

I know journalists who have operated with great success for three decades or more without ever doing a bit of work that could be called investigative with a capital I. They are the norm.

4. The Myth of the Journalist as Defender of Freedom

There is, of course, some basis for this myth, as for the others, but the weight of evidence runs the other way. There have been times when individual journalists have fought long, successful battles for freedom, but there have been other times—many more—when journalism saw its essential duty to be to run with the pack.

When Senator Joseph McCarthy was mounting his one-man reign of terror in the United States, most of the press spent most of its time getting on side. Indeed, McCarthy had no instrument more powerful than a credulous press for the advancement of his bizarre view of the world. With rare exceptions, as dissent, free speech, and the right to privacy of opinion were smashed to the ground, the major elements of the press either went along, or kept their heads down and their mouths shut.

It was not journalists who sat in at lunch counters in Montgomery, Alabama, or marched down the main street of Selma, or enrolled to vote in Jackson, Mississippi. What the press did was to cover the activities of those who were, in fact, the defenders of freedom. It was a key role, but it was not the role of standing in the line of battle.

When journalism does take on that role, as the *New York Times* did in the Pentagon Papers case, it does so slowly, reluctantly, with many doubts and misgivings. In his account, Harrison Salisbury quotes A. M. Rosenthal, saying of the Pentagon Papers report, "I don't want to see it published, but it must be published." The line does not have the same ring as "Give me liberty or give me death," but it is a true and fair reflection of the attitude of responsible journalists.

The press in the United States is far more concerned, far more aggressive in the defense of its own rights and those of others than the press in Canada, where there has always been what one American writer calls "an automatic deference to authority." When, in October 1970, the Liberal government of Pierre Elliott Trudeau, responding to an "apprehended insurrection" for which no convincing evidence has ever been forthcoming, imposed the War Measures Act and sent troops into Montreal and Ottawa, the overwhelming response of the press was enthusiastic and prolonged applause. When more than four hundred citizens were rounded up, arrested, and thrown into jail, without charge or warrant, and held there without bail or legal advice, beyond the reach of any writ of habeas corpus, the press thundered its approbation. And, when the government clamped rules on all the media to ensure that no dissenting or provocative comments would disturb the gunpoint calm, not one newspaper, radio station, or television network ever challenged the government's right to wipe out fundamental liberties with the stroke of a pen. It became a crime in Canada ever to have belonged to the Front de Libération du Québec, a legal organization until the War Measures Act was imposed; and even this retroactive law failed to arouse the media.

I like to believe that in the United States, someone, somewhere in journalism, would have raised the challenge which was never forthcoming in Canada; but perhaps that is wishful thinking on my part.

5. The Myth of the Journalist as Friend of the Little People

Over the mantel on the fireplace in the Parliamentary Press Gallery in Ottawa there is carved a legend which instructs that the task of journalism is to "comfort the afflicted and afflict the comfortable." A noble sentiment, but if I were one of the afflicted, I wouldn't try to cash it at the bank.

It does happen on occasion that a newspaper or radio or television station takes up the cause of someone oppressed by some jack-in-office or corporate goon. Such stories make good fodder; they are full of human interest. But they run counter to the general practice of reporting, which consists of telling us what the Worthwhile People are saying and doing, how they dress, what they read, where they eat, with whom they sleep—sometimes, even how often—and what they think. The columns of a newspaper and the microphones of radio and television are generally available to the rich and righteous and only occasionally to the poor and pitiable. What a tycoon says is news; what you and I say is noise. If you want to test this thesis for yourself, put out a press release the day Henry Kissinger condescends to unveil his latest plan to sort out the planet, and see which of you gets the better play in the media. You may have more worthwhile and more truthful words to say than Kissinger—I can hardly imagine otherwise—but that will not be your phiz on the evening news, it will be Henry's.

It is not the Little People whose views are sought on the financial pages of your daily newspaper. In fact, that section is devoted to quoting, applauding, and reassuring corporation executives, would-be executives, and stockmarket touts. Every day these worthies find their views embodied in print, their prejudices reaffirmed, their scorn of government interference echoed, their demands for more government subsidies solemnized. It is the newspaper's not unreasonable hope that a business community so cosseted will respond by placing ads in the newspaper. And so, by golly, it will.

The rest of the journal is only marginally different. On page one, we are treated to what an automobile company president thinks should be done to turn the economy around; on page three, to what a union leader wants done about foreign imports; and on the entertainment page, to a rock star's recipe for goulash and universal peace.

There is no section for the bums, deadbeats, unemployed, helpless, hopeless, and handicapped. If we are to be treated to the views of a neighborhood barber, plumber, or mechanic, it will be in a feature roped off from the rest of the paper and called "On the Street" or "What People are Saying," with head and shoulder pictures and one-line responses to such searing questions as: "Should Reagan Grow a Moustache?"

There is nothing remarkable about the fact that journalists concentrate on the movers and shakers. You cannot sell newspapers, or television spots, on the basis of what Blotz the Butcher is up to. The only remarkable thing is that journalists should waste time and effort holding themselves out as champions of the underdog. They are for the overdog, always have been, always will be.

The only new development in this line is the emergence, especially in the United States, of the journalist as overdog. Television cameras flash to the front of an elegant mansion in Georgetown, and from the assembled limousines the movers and shakers disembark, nodding affably to the assembled multitudes. Ripe politicians are noted with awe, along with overripe business tycoons, lobbyists, and consultants. Pushing in with this crowd come the media stars—but in fact there is only one medium that counts at this level of public exposure, and that is television. The commentator notes the presence of David Brinkley with every bit as much awe as that of, say, Gerald Ford, Henry Kissinger, or George Bush.

The journalist as celebrity is not entirely new—H. L. Mencken filled both roles, and so did Walter Lippmann—but, in an earlier age, it was the journalist's established skill over a period of years that brought celebrity. Today, fame is instantly available, and often on no firmer basis than possession of a deep voice, striking looks, or a sincere hairdo. What is particularly disturbing is that the glamour-pusses have become the role models for journalists. Don't bother me with tedious tales of wrongs done to Indians; what I want is a contract that says the studio has to send a limo around to pick me up for work. Some of the Western world's most admired journalists would not know an underdog if it bit them on the ankle, although they may be terrific at registering compassion on camera.

6. The Fourth Estate Myth

I blame Thomas Jefferson for this myth; Jefferson and Thomas Carlyle. It was Jefferson who said: "Were it left for me to decide whether we should have a government without newspapers, or newspapers without a government, I should not hesitate a moment to prefer the latter." A silly, pretentious comment to make, even in Jefferson's time. What role did he see for himself? Editor-in-chief? With Sally Hemings as a copy-girl? What does it mean, anyway? Is a civilization conceivable in which there would be no police, hospitals, public highways, or sewer systems—except by private fiat—but a civilization that would swarm with the *Toledo Blade,* the *New York Post,* and the *National Enquirer?*

Jefferson's puffery was made worse when Carlyle penned his famous line about "the Stupendous Fourth Estate," to which he gave great credit for fomenting and carrying out the French Revolution. Between them, Jefferson and Carlyle managed to give generations of journalists the notion that they were a branch of government, and not the least important branch, either.

Journalists still believe this myth. During the hearings of the Royal Commission on Newspapers in Canada, Michael Sifton, a western publisher, laid this line on the commissioners: "We have a democracy because we have a free press. We don't have a free press because we have a democracy." Stick that in your pipe and smoke it, Jean Jacques Rousseau.

Why did the barons force King John to sign the Magna Carta? Leading columnists of the day pushed them into it.

How did we get habeas corpus? It came on the heels of a stinging editorial in the *London Daily Mail* of 1314.

What did Charles the First say when they hauled him to the chopping block? "I should never have cancelled my subscription to *News of the World*."

Journalists are in the information-processing business, a business they share with many others, including politicians, authors, race-track tipsters, advertisers, computer programmers, bureaucrats, educators, clergymen, and snake-oil salesmen. They are not the sole custodians of information—which would, in fact, make them a branch of government—and they are certainly not the sole custodians of democracy.

It is the role of journalists to explore, to explain, and, sometimes, to challenge the world around them. It is not their role to arrange or to rearrange that world, and they are at their worst when they step out of the job for which alone they possess the required competence.

The United States has a custom that sorts out this business, the presidential press conference. Even for inept presidents, even for a Gerald Ford or a Jimmy Carter, the presidential press conference is a walkover, because everyone—the press, the president, the onlookers—understands that the journalist is not, and should not be, on the same footing as the nation's highest elected official. The president receives his mandate from the voter, the legitimate repository of power. The journalists have no mandate but their mouths, and a contest between the two is seldom informative or edifying.

In Canada, although we have press conferences with the prime minister—they are a walkover for him, too—we also have the daily scrum called the parliamentary question period, when members of Parliament of every shade and stripe can get up on their hind legs and question, poke, prod, and even insult the leader of Her Majesty's government. The prime minister doesn't like being called to account this way, but he has to put up with it. The daily question period provides a constant, glaring light on the affairs of the nation. It is my guess that, if Americans had had such an institution in this country, President Nixon would have been forced out of office at least a year earlier than he was. But question period works because it matches equal to equal—or very nearly—and puts the journalists back in their proper role as observers, conduits, and commentators. It leaves the role of wrestling for power to those elected for the task, and relieves the journalists of the imposing but improbable role thrust on them by Jefferson and Carlyle.

7. The Myth of Professionalism

"Journalism," according to the report of the Royal Commission on Newspapers in Canada, "has as its philosophical ideal the quest for what is true and right." For all I know, this ideal may be dead on, although I don't believe most journalists would recognize a philosophical ideal if you handed it to them on a platter, with watercress around it. Truth and right are fine, and I applaud them, but I have never attended a page one conference at which the managing editor asked, "Which truth deserves the black line today?" or "What right are we featuring below the fold?"

The usual goals of journalism have always lain somewhere between the vision of the British press baron, Lord Beaverbrook, who said that his purpose was "to make propaganda," and the vision of most publishers, which is to make money, or, failing that, just to survive. At the top, money, power, and influence are the jackpots in journalism, not truth and right, whatever they may be this week.

Journalism is, in short, an industry, marked by the same skill, zeal, greed, imagination, aptitude, hope, drive, ineptitude, energy, and idealism as, say, the manufacture of ballpoint pens. It is more important than manufacturing ballpoint pens only because its product, information, has more general value.

But what journalism is not is a profession, particularly a profession driven by the vision of a holy grail. A profession requires, among all else, a set of standards for training, licensing, and continued practice. I, a journalist for thirty years, have never taken a course in journalism, never written an examination in the subject, never held a license, never had to prove to anyone, except the people who hired me—and, from time to time, the people who sued me—that I knew what I was doing. If I practiced medicine for thirty years, chances are that at the end of that time I would have a good notion of how to cut people up, but that would not make me a doctor. Journalists swear no oaths, subscribe to no code of ethics, carry no certificate of competence that can be challenged or revoked. They may—it is not usual, but they may—be subject to the rulings of a press council or an ombudsman, but by and large a journalist is a journalist, and remains one because he says he is, and has been able to persuade someone to print his stuff.

The people who labor for the *National Enquirer* are journalists, and may be better paid than they who breathe the rarified air of the *New York Times*. The practitioner whose sole training consisted of snitching on classmates in school will be admitted to the same press conference as someone who has a doctorate from the Columbia School of Journalism.

It has become the norm on newspapers that the people who are hired have taken at least a course in journalism, and that they are paid a premium if they have a graduate degree in the subject. I am not sure that these people make better journalists, but their enrolling in the subject shows at least an interest. This is not the same as following a profession.

There has been a move in recent years to regularize the craft, to set up standards, to draw up codes of ethics, to press for some system of monitoring the performance of journalists. I am all for it, as long as it doesn't go too far. It is not that I object to being judged or held responsible, or even to the notion that I and my colleagues should have to show some minimal competence before we are turned loose on the world. My concern is that journalism is already too big for its britches. Give us a national college of journalism, with an ethics committee and a review board and a licensing panel; and, even if we can avoid the censorship and intimidation such a situation invites, we will be in a hell of a mess. The hallmarks of our professionalism will legitimize the highfalutin notions that already threaten to turn the tribe of ink-stained wretches into a collegium.

In French Canada, journalists have already formed themselves, somewhat in the European tradition, into what could loosely be called a quasi-profession through their unions. In Quebec, journalists have argued—and on two occasions struck—for a share in the formation of news policy and editorial policy. At *Le Devoir,* Canada's most prestigious French-language paper, they have won such a share outright, and they have won partial victories at *Le Soleil* in Quebec City and at *La Presse* in Montreal. They regard themselves as much more than mere communicators; they are pamphleteers, instructors, and molders of society.

In his article, "French Journalism in Quebec: Solidarity on a Pedestal," in the volume of essays I edited, *Canadian Newspapers: The Inside Story,* Dominique Clift, a journalist who has worked in both English and French journalism, explains the difference between English and French journalists in Canada:

> It is in the actual practice of journalism that French and English
> writers differ in the most pronounced manner. It has to do with
> the way in which journalists look upon themselves, their profes-
> sion [note that he calls it a profession], and their public, as well as
> on their employers. French journalists see for themselves a much
> more exalted role in society than do their English-speaking coun-
> terparts. This attitude has become much more noticeable during

the last twenty years or so. . . . Favourable changes in labour legislation have provided unprecedented opportunities for upwardly-mobile people in various intellectual occupations in which education is a prime consideration. In addition to greater financial rewards, unionism has brought some educated occupational groups, such as journalists and teachers, a type of group solidarity and power which was once characteristic only of doctors and lawyers . . . and priests.

Clift goes on to argue that French-Canadian journalists, in moving themselves into a professional mode like that of doctors and lawyers, were in danger of wrecking their own craft. He is right, I believe, and for that reason, while I have always applauded any steps to make journalism a more responsible and better-trained trade, I have always shied away from any movement that would either recognize journalism as a profession in being, or try to make it into one.

In the United States, the yearning for professionalism has emerged in a different and probably healthier way in the plethora of institutions, centers, schools, consultative groups, and consultants who assemble across the broad land to study journalism. Learned treatises pour out of the universities; questionnaires flutter through the air; sociologists, clutching grants from foundations, wrinkle their brows over such vexed issues as What Is Bias? (to which the answer is simple: bias is disagreement with me). All good clean stuff, which compels both journalists and others to think about the craft and how it operates. The only danger that may arise is when all these people with all these grants to work on convince themselves that what they are studying is a profession—otherwise, why so much fuss? It is not a profession, and the first thing those who would analyze journalism should be taught is to bring to its study the qualities that make it worthwhile as a craft: curiosity, intelligence, and skepticism.

In outlining the seven myths of journalism, I hope I have not left the impression that I dislike my calling or that I am ashamed of it. *Au contraire*. Most of the time, I find working as a journalist the most exciting, interesting, engaging work to be found on the surface of the globe. Some days I cannot believe I get paid to do what I do—which is to find things out and to write. But three decades have taught me the limitations of that craft, as well as its central strength, which is to try to see things as they are, and not as we might wish them to be. Edward Verrall Lucas—no journalist—once asked the really tough question for any of us in this business. "Has any reader," he asked, "ever found perfect accuracy in the newspaper account of any event of which he had inside knowledge?" I doubt it, and as long as I doubt it, I think it important for journalists to concern themselves with the reality of their business, rather than to spend their time burnishing its myths.

Robert Kroetsch

Canadian Writing: No Name Is My Name

In a new place, and in its literature, the Adamic impulse to give name asserts itself, as it did in the New England of Emerson and Thoreau and Hawthorne. Writers in a new place conceive of themselves profoundly as namers. They name in order to give focus and definition. They name to create boundaries. They name to establish identity.

Canadian writing is the writing down of a new place. Indeed, Northrop Frye tells us in his now famous statement that the Canadian sensibility "is less perplexed by the question 'Who am I?' than by some such riddle as 'Where is here?'"

Frye's insight is basic to the unriddling of whatever it is to be a Canadian. Yet it slights a question that is at least manifest, if not central. The interest in the question of identity speaks its presence in a curious way. That presence announces itself as an absence. Or, more specifically, one of the peculiarities of this new literature is the recurrence of major fictional characters who have no names.

This resistance to a speakable name occurs early in Canadian writing. Thomas Haliburton, in a series of newspaper pieces begun in 1835 in Nova Scotia and published together in 1836 under the title *The Clockmaker,* invented the willful and eloquent character to whom he gave the name Sam Slick. That same Sam Slick, that first great Canadian literary character, is not a Bluenose at all but, rather, a New Englander, a Yankee clockmaker. The narrator of the story, the incipient Canadian (this is before Confederation) refuses to name himself.

The two men travel together on horseback as they ride circuit, one a clock peddler, the other a lawyer. (And travel itself is, of course, a form of escape from name; Canadian writing is obsessively about travel.) On this ride, Sam Slick does most of the talking. The other man tells about the talking; he is at once at a remove from the action and its mediator. And he is, by fascinating design, anonymous.

We are in Episode eleven before the matter of his anonymity is confronted. It is suppertime. The narrator is approached by the hostess of Pugwash's inn: "Approaching me, she said, with an irresistible smile, 'Would you like, Mr. —' Here there was a pause, a hiatus, evidently intended for me to fill up with my name."

The irresistible smile of the hostess is, it turns out, resistible. And the narrator gives us a longish paragraph on why. He says of his name:

> but that no person knows, nor do I intend they shall; at Medley's Hotel, in Halifax, I was known as the Stranger in No. 1. The attention that incognito procured for me, the importance it gave me in the eyes of the master of the house, its lodgers and servants, is indescribable. It is only great people who travel incog.

He names himself by giving a name that leaves him nameless. He is, or was, the Stranger in No. 1. But even that was somewhere else, not here in Pugwash's inn. This narrator has discovered a version of privilege in anonymity. He is not above a little deceit. His delight is almost naive. But the lawyer-impulse in the narrator makes him attempt at least a partial description of the indescribable: "State travelling is inconvenient and slow; the constant weight of form and etiquette oppresses at once the strength and the spirits. It is pleasant to travel unobserved, to stand at ease, or exchange the full suit for the undress coat and fatigue jacket."

The man who wants to be recognized for his importance wants also to go unobserved. This comes close to contradiction. We see here an early manifestation of the Canadian personality. The man who exploits social hierarchy by being falsely named into it wants also to be free of it. He wants to have a system that gives him identity and stature, but he wants to be free of that system. This man is surely ready to enter into the Canadian Confederation. Having created his own coffin and climbed into it, he now manages, by some wonderful sleight of hand, to nail it shut:

> Wherever, too, there is mystery there is importance; there is no knowing for whom I may be mistaken; but let me once give my humble cognomen and occupation, and I sink immediately to my own level, to a plebian station, and a vulgar name; not even my beautiful hostess, nor my inquisitive friend, the Clockmaker, who calls me "Squire," shall extract that secret!

This remarkable and sort-of anonymous man fears that by naming himself accurately he will, in a mind-boggling paradox, sink immediately to his own level. Perhaps this is at the heart of the enduring Canadian crisis about the federal state: I would never join a country that would have me as a member.

It is better, much more desirable, the narrator insists, to be *mistaken*. And yet this same narrator is fascinated by—captivated by —the person who admits to and even proclaims for himself a plebian station and a vulgar name.

Sam Slick is the double and opposite of Haliburton's narrator. He is the named man who fearlessly and proudly, and with his own kind of shrewdness, speaks his own name. For all his "soft sawder," Sam speaks direct truths. He is, in a certain way, the carnivalesque destroyer of the hierarchy which the narrator both admires and wishes to escape. He deals in actual clocks and profane time and the randomness and the chance and the poetry at the edge of *law*. The nameless narrator meets his alter ego and both hankers for the freedom of Sam's sly directness and clings to the legalistic indirectness of his own being "incog." Not even his beautiful hostess, he tells (and her charms, he lets us know, in an extravagant fit of naming, are like an Italian sky, unclouded, unrivaled), nor the inquisitive Clockmaker who, with soft sawder that is usually effective, calls him Squire, "shall extract the secret!"

That secret remains a recurring theme in Canadian writing. Haliburton announces it and complicates it. His narrator, who is the Stranger in No. 1 and the mystery and the Squire, is also Haliburton. That trace of the autobiographical is to persist in later renderings of the nameless figure. Haliburton is himself, astonishingly, the man of law—lawyer and judge—creating at once the carnivalesque energy of Sam Slick and the contained lawlessness of his status-seeking narrator. Haliburton himself, when he could no longer live with his own contradiction, his own tension, his own dialogic involvement, went to England and became a member of Parliament and opposed the movement of the British North American colonies toward independence. And in his later writings, in a further bizarre paradox, he turned against his own character, Sam Slick, as if that character must be a real person and not his creation.

But Haliburton, in his first "refusing to name" scene, was brilliantly aware of the ironies of his posture. "Would you like, Mr. ——" the narrator quotes again, after his own longish digression. And then he continues to narrate the incident:

> "Indeed, I would," said I, "Mrs. Pugwash; pray be seated, and tell me what it is."
>
> "Would you like a dish of superior Shittyacks for supper?"
>
> "Indeed I would," said I, again, laughing: "but pray tell me what it is?"
>
> "Laws me!" said she with a stare. "Where have you been all your days, that you never heerd of our Shittyack oysters? I thought everybody had heerd of them."

The man who withholds his name himself comes to a name that for him names nothing. Haliburton sees, comically, the necessary and absurd implications both of naming and of his own refusal to name. He is, there in 1835, the writer, the namer, in the new world, come to the old genesis problem, the old genesis moment. Where Melville's narrator could speak so richly and powerfully, "Call me Ishmael," Haliburton's narrator could only insist, with ambiguous laughter, on having no name.

If we look to the invisible characters in American writing, the invisible man, or the voice that says "nobody knows my name," those are the voices of people who feel they are being made nameless by others. The Canadian narrator makes him- or herself invisible. And that Canadian is often, as was Haliburton's narrator, from the dominant force or class in society.

The paradigmatic text in Canadian writing may be Sinclair Ross's 1941 novel, *As for Me and My House*. In the opening of that novel a minister and his wife are newly arrived and unpacking in the small prairie town of Horizon. It is typical of Canadian writing that the stranger or intruder who enters the small community is not a cowboy or an outlaw or an otherwise disreputable figure, but rather a figure of authority—often a teacher, sometimes a minister or a doctor.

The prairie world of Ross's novel is without boundaries—instead of a boundary it is crossed by a railway that suggests a meaningless infinity. The name of the town, Horizon, suggests a no-place that is tantalizingly visible but always out of reach: a version of namelessness.

Mr. and Mrs. Bentley move into a nondescript house of their own, and are hardly ever seen in the house next door where God seems to be either too often absent or too often ignored—and seldom named.

The novel is presented in the form of Mrs. Bentley's diary. This fascinating woman, while keeping something as intimate as a diary, never reveals to us her first name, her maiden name, or her family background. We know at best that she once entertained thoughts of a career in music—and hers is a version of European music that does not transport a lot of personal information. It serves almost to elaborate her disguise or her fate, her condition of namelessness.

This same "nameless" Mrs. Bentley—and that is our name for her; she toys with the stereotype of "minister's wife" but won't name herself as such—is quite possibly the most discussed fictional character in Canadian writing. She, in a sense, writes about an unwritten novel which we as readers must imagine or reconstruct while reading her diary entries about the missing text; the novel itself as a larger act of naming is called into doubt.

Mrs. Bentley, while carefully not naming herself, with equal care explores and records the names of all the people and even the animals around her. A major figure in Mrs. Bentley's diary, the schoolteacher Paul Kirby, is an amateur etymologist and philologist so caught up in the meaning of names that he cannot get beyond them to people. Her husband Philip, the minister, after taking in a stray dog, bathes it in a mock-baptism (naming), and Mrs. Bentley reports carefully that "the drowned-looking Philip named him [the dog] El Greco—because El Greco was an artist who had a way of painting people long and lean as if they'd all been put on the rack." While on a potentially Edenic vacation on a ranch she notices a picture of a Hereford over her bed and writes in her diary:

> I looked at him [that is the Hereford, not the husband; he is absent] closer when I got up today, and found that his name was Gallant Lad the Third. His son, Annie tells me, is here now on the ranch and carrying on. As a calf, though, he belonged to Paul, and instead of Gallant Lad the Fourth he's Priapus the First.

This might be a clue to the paternity of the fatherless son who is born to a dying mother, Judith West, and adopted by the Bentleys. But it also reduces naming to a kind of absurdity. And the novel ends with still another ambiguous naming act, when Mrs. Bentley names the adopted baby boy, Philip. "Another Philip?" her husband, Philip, protests. "That's right, Philip," she replies. "I want it so."

Mrs. Bentley will settle for either too little or too much naming. But she won't herself be named. Like Haliburton's narrator, she engages in vast and devious verbal design to give herself at least margins of freedom, while finding herself tagged as the minister's helpmate in a claustrophobic small town on a limitless prairie. She names her world in great detail in order to keep herself nameless. She is the taboo-keeper, not of God's name, but of her own. Perhaps she is first of all a nameless figure in her husband's world, but she wins through that preserved and nurtured namelessness a complex humanity.

That rural or small-town setting—not the wilderness, but its edge—somehow remains the basic place of Canadian fiction, as if there must be a doubt even about where the place is. Place threatens to become mere space. From Susanna Moodie's *Roughing It in the Bush* to Ernest Buckler's *The Mountain and the Valley,* from Sheila Watson's *The Double Hook* to Margaret Laurence's *The Diviners* and Jack Hodgins's *The Invention of the World,* there is a resistance to centers. The rural or small-town setting remains the test place, the energy source, for those sophisticated writers. They are all tempted to set their stories in "Horizon." Nature itself becomes an undeciphered text as the old names fall away or prove to be inadequate or false. And with that emptiness at the center of sign comes the feeling of guilt about our innocence that is so characteristic of Canadian writing.

We do, of course, have in our canon urban novels. Quite possibly the best of all is A. M. Klein's 1951 novel *The Second Scroll.* Klein was a Montreal writer who had a distinguished career as a poet, as a political activist, as a student of Joyce, and as a lawyer. The narrator of his only novel is a Jewish-Canadian writer-journalist who goes to Europe on a double quest. And that narrator is nameless.

He is sent to Israel by a publisher to produce "a volume of translations of the poems and songs of Israel's latest nest of singing birds." That is, he is to investigate the emergence of a literature newer even than Canada's; and again, as in Canada, there is a vast prior literature to confront. But the nameless narrator is also in search of an uncle, Uncle Melech, a great but mysterious Hebrew scholar.

The novel begins (and the first chapter is called "Genesis"): "For many years my father—may he dwell in bright Eden!—refused to permit in his presence even the mention of that person's name." The narrator realizes that in order to seek his uncle he must engage in a naming act that assumes the proportions of a taboo-breaking. Again, the old names must somehow be made new, and the person assigned the task, the person assigned to mediate the transformation (as in Ross's novel), never reveals his own name, almost as if he had none to reveal.

Against this potentially tragic assignment, Klein plays his sense of the new-naming and the mis-naming that are a part of the contemporary urban world. In the process of finding a Catholic monsignor in Rome who knows something of Uncle Melech, Klein's narrator meets Settano, a "polylingual autodidact." The narrator reports:

> When after several Scotch and sodas I had ordered—out of pure thirst and nostalgia—a Coke . . . , he had scoffed at me, styled me a typical emissary of the new religion, a sound, orthodox Cocacolian. I had spitefully accepted the compliment and . . . had expatiated upon the beauty of the Coca-Cola bottle, curved and dusky like some Gauguin painting of a South Sea maiden, upon the purity of its contents, its ubiquity in space, its symbolic evocations—a little torchless Statue of Liberty.

He continues in that parody of his own quest:

> . . . and the evening had ended with a quasi-friendship, both of us at last quaffing it down with Canadian V.O. As an abbreviation, he said, for vodka. He then bade me good night, *Americano.*
> "I am not an American. I'm a Canadian."
> "Is there a difference? Isn't Canada the forty-ninth state?"
> "On the contrary. The States are our eleventh province."
> His laughter—the gall of the Canuck! the utter absurdity!—rang through the corridor.

Klein has an overwhelming sense of the sacred and the profane, of the political and the personal implications of namelessness. His long silence at the end of his life is a painful statement of that awareness. On the one hand he could imagine, through renaming, wide ecumenical possibilities, as he does in the glosses at the end of his novel. On the other hand he saw that we cannot name our brands of booze with any sense of conviction. He could imagine the English and the French and the Jewish communities of Montreal living in harmony, yet he entertained profound doubts about the notion of the self as something whole and realizable in the urban world. He anticipates contemporary anxieties about the very notion of self, and he grounds that anxiety in a nameless narrator who goes in quest of a figure whose name is not to be mentioned. In the course of conducting that search, both Klein and his narrator move through varieties of discourse, including within the one short novel varieties of the poem, of the play, of the essay, of the gloss—not to mention a variety of languages. When the narrator finally finds at least a snapshot of his missing uncle, it turns out to be "a double, a multiple exposure." There is no longer, in Klein's world, the possibility of a simple and definitive naming.

In that same Montreal, fourteen years after the appearance of *The Second Scroll,* Hubert Aquin was to publish in French his novel *Prochain Episode.* And again, it is a novel whose narrator-hero has no name.

Where Klein's hero was on a double quest, the nameless narrator in *Prochain Episode* is at least a double agent in his own story. He is in a Montreal prison, but has been transferred to a clinic where he is to be, as he puts it, "submitted to psychiatric expertise before being sent to trial." In this condition of enforced stasis he writes a story of a frantic trip through Switzerland where he was attempting to serve Quebec's revolutionary cause by killing another double agent, a well-to-do historian who is the narrator's own double.

This book, along with being about time and history and Quebec and revolution, is about the writing act itself. We read on the first page:

> At heart, only one problem occupies me: how should I set about writing a story of espionage? And I complicate the problem with my dream of doing something original in a field encumbered by a great many written and unwritten rules. Fortunately, laziness immediately persuades me to give up any thought of reshaping the espionage format. I also feel great security, I confess, in gently yielding to the demands of a literary style already so well defined. So I decide to slip my novel into the mainstream of the spy-story tradition.

He lays claim even to the anonymity of authorship that is offered by an adherence to convention. He grounds that anonymity in a philosophic claim that originality is no longer possible and, in any case, only barely desirable. He says, later in the story, "It's no longer a matter of how to be original in literature: suddenly I am disillusioned by the question of individual existence!"

Process has replaced end in a radical way, as the title of Aquin's book would suggest. The narrator says: "The meaning of this novel will not be the shattering novelty of its final format. I am this book from hour to hour and day to day; as long as I don't commit suicide, I have no intention of stopping. This disorderly book and I, we are the same."

The narrator and the book are one in a process that borders on dissolution. Aquin has written a successful description of a total failure—his book becomes the synonym for a character who is not only nameless but who finds himself unnameable.

Yet this version of anonymity generates story. There can only be the next episode, and this is possible because every character or event divides, turns against itself, doubles back on itself—Switzerland becomes a double and a contrary to Quebec; Quebec becomes its Eastern Townships and its St. Lawrence River; the victim gives the same account of his life as did the would-be murderer; the blonde woman K (or Quebec) sought after and longed for by the narrator might be the blonde woman K (or Quebec) sought after and longed for by the historian and scholar H. de Heutz, who might be the banker Carl von Ryndt.

Writing, the narrator says, wins time: "dead time which I cover with erasures and phonemes, which I embellish with syllables and bravado, which I shower with all my atoms, fragments of a whole they will never equal. I write automatically, concentrating on spelling to avoid the compelling logic of homicide."

Aquin's hero finds in his namelessness a prison and a destiny, a defeat and a cause, a way of writing and a reason not to write. Aquin himself took his own life in 1977—he postponed his suicide by a day when his wife said the day he had chosen would be inconvenient for her. Aquin was true to his fictional vision. The intertext of suicide is in his books. He blurred the distinction between book and life. He entered into his own narrative of unnameability.

It remained for Margaret Atwood, in her 1972 novel *Surfacing*, to test urban Canadian characters in a rural Canadian setting. Atwood's heroine and narrator in *Surfacing* is an Everywoman figure come to an archetypal confrontation with parental figures, with garden and forest, with the city of the present and the totemic creatures of the past. The nameless narrator begins her story: "I can't believe I'm on this road again, twisting along past the lake where the white birches are dying, the disease is spreading from the south, and I notice they now have sea-planes for hire. But this is still near the city limits; we didn't go through, it's swelled enough to have a bypass, that's success."

This woman harks back to Haliburton's narrator: she is like him a city person gone into the country; she is aware of a stronger sense of definition that comes up from the south and, like Haliburton's narrator, she is attracted to and suspicious of one of those defining characteristics—success.

Atwood's character enters into a labyrinth where she has not even the reassurance of her own name. Instead of a quest for a fixed and knowable and bounded identity in the labyrinth of the world, we have the idea of identity itself as the labyrinth. Like Aquin's hero, Atwood's narrator risks being destroyed and has experienced the desire to kill. Like Ross's heroine, she finds in the (now imagined) paternity of a child a locus for her obsession: an awareness of the possibility and impossibility of connecting name and object, of putting a name on things.

Atwood's four travelers in their car enter into Quebec. The narrator says, "Now we're on my home ground, foreign territory." There is not even the consolation of home as a safe place for this narrator. She returns home and sees the familiar signs in a language she cannot quite read. She meets the people she has "known" for a long time and cannot quite speak with. In Quebec, on "my home ground, foreign territory," she is, like Aquin's narrator, only made aware of a larger failure of language to name, to signify.

"Nothing," she says, "is the same, I don't know the way any more." And yet she is, like Aquin's narrator, the figure of the artist. The artist is supposed to know the way. She too, like Aquin's narrator, is the artist at the edge of dissolution. "I can't believe . . ." is the cry of her beginning. At the end of the book she frees herself of history, of clothing, of artifacts like scrapbooks and photographs and wedding rings. Only when she has made herself unnameable in any traditional terms can she begin what might be a rebirth, a renaming into a valid vision or version of the world.

One comes reluctantly, uneasily, to the question: What is this anonymity all about? What is the name for what is not named?

Perhaps Atwood's heroine is a new Eve, freeing herself from Adam's named world. It may well be that Canadian writing owes its first debt to the model of Eve, and not to that of Adam. Eve is created into the world after Adam has been created—and after the naming has been done.

The Canadian writer in English must speak a new culture not with new names but with an abundance of names inherited from Britain and the United States. And that predicament is in turn doubled—by the writing done in the French language in Canada.

The problem then is not so much that of knowing one's identity as it is that of how to relate that newly evolving identity to its inherited or "given" names. And the first technique might be simply to hold those names in suspension, to let the identity speak itself out of a willed namelessness.

The experience of feeling powerless might also be a factor in the Canadian sense of being nameless. American literature is powerfully grounded in its nineteenth-century greatness, in the implications and assumptions of American Romanticism. Canadian literature is very much a literature of the later twentieth century. The nineteenth century gave American literature special interests in and definitions of self, freedom, heroism, society, nature, happiness. The twentieth century, as the basis of Canadian writing, puts special pressure on all those concepts. It would be illuminating to contrast the "I" of Whitman that can encompass the world with the "I" of bpNichol's long poem, *The Martyrology,* an "I" that yields itself to the encompassing world.

In Canadian writing, and perhaps in Canadian life, there is an exceptional pressure placed on the individual and the self by the community or society. The self is not in any way Romantic or privileged. The small town remains the ruling paradigm, with its laws of familiarity and conformity. Self and community almost fight to a draw. There seems to be little literature in Canada that tells of the small-town person going to the city—a tradition that is strong in European and American literature. The principal character in Shelia Watson's *The Double Hook* kills his mother, goes into town to a place where he might catch a train and leave—and then he turns around and rides back to the community in which he committed the murder. David Canaan in Ernest Buckler's *The Mountain and the Valley* gets into the car that would take him away from his small town and into the city—then gets out of the car and stays. The pressure of community at its strongest—or worst—is toward erasure.

But at its best, the threat of anonymity generates story. Aquin makes a labyrinthine novel of his hero's inability to fix on a name. Sinclair Ross's narrator writes a commentary on a novel that we don't have (her husband's silence) and in the process writes the basic Canadian story. Morag Gunn, that busy, troubled, interrupted, procrastinating woman in Margaret Laurence's *The Diviners,* raised as an orphan and threatened with that version of namelessness, insists over and over that she can't get her work done, isn't getting her novel written, can't in effect put a name to her experience—and we end up having finished reading the novel just as she finishes writing it.

It may well be that the villain (namelessness) turns out to be the hero in the story of the Canadian story. The nameless figure who seems to threaten us may in fact be leading us to high ground. To avoid a name does not (as Haliburton's narrator so well realized) deprive one of an identity; indeed, it may offer a plurality of identities. Like the epic hero of old, we might even lay claim to a certain virtue in our ability to withhold and deceive. In a willful misremembering of Homer's Odysseus we might say, ambiguously, proudly, tauntingly, no name is *my* name!

About the Authors

MONIQUE BÉGIN, Chair of Women's Studies at the University of Ottawa and Carleton University, was born in Rome, Italy, in 1936. She received her B.A. (1958) and M.A. (1961) from the Université de Montréal, and pursued further postgraduate studies at the Université de Paris (Sorbonne). She was Executive Secretary of the Royal Commission on the Status of Women (1967–70) and Assistant Director of Research, Canadian Radio-television and Telecommunications Commission (1970–72). In 1972 she was elected federal member of Parliament for the Liberal party in the riding of St-Michel (Montreal), the first woman from Quebec elected to the House of Commons. She was Minister of National Revenue (1976–77) and Minister of National Health and Welfare (1977–79; 1980–84). In 1984–85 she was Visiting G. Schaefer Professor of Economics, University of Notre Dame. She has received honorary degrees from St. Thomas University (1977) and Mount Saint Vincent University (1982).

THOMAS R. BERGER, Professor of Law, University of British Columbia, was born in Victoria, British Columbia, in 1933. He received his B.A. (1955) and LL.D. (1956) from the University of British Columbia. In 1962–63 he was federal member of Parliament for the New Democratic Party in the riding of Vancouver-Burrard and, in 1966–69, provincial member of the Legislative Assembly for the New Democratic Party in the same riding. In 1971 he was named to the Supreme Court of British Columbia, the youngest appointee to the Court in this century; he served as judge until 1983. He was Chairman of the British Columbia Royal Commission on Family and Children's Law (1973–75), Commissioner of the Mackenzie Valley Pipeline Inquiry (1974–77), and Commissioner of the Alaska Native Review Commission (1983–85). He is the author of *Northern Frontier, Northern Homeland: The Report of the Mackenzie Valley Pipe-*

line Inquiry (1977), *Fragile Freedoms: Human Rights and Dissent in Canada* (1981), and *Village Journey: The Report of the Alaska Native Review Commission* (1985). He has received honorary degrees from the University of Notre Dame at Nelson, B.C. (1975), York University (1977), University of Manitoba (1978), Saint Thomas University (1979), University of Waterloo (1979), Simon Fraser University (1979), University of Victoria (1980), Queen's University (1980), University of Guelph (1984), Trent University (1984), and University of Saskatchewan (1985).

JUDY EROLA was born in Sudbury, Ontario, in 1934. An interviewer and commentator for many years in radio and television, she participated in many aspects of the broadcasting field, both before the cameras and behind the scenes in business and management. In 1980 she was elected federal member of Parliament for the Liberal party in the riding of Nickel Belt (Sudbury area) and immediately appointed Minister of State (Mines). In 1981 she was handed the additional portfolio of Status of Women Canada. She was the first woman to serve on the Priorities and Planning Committee of Cabinet. In 1983 she was appointed Minister of Consumer and Corporate Affairs, retaining her role as Minister Responsible for the Status of Women. In 1984 she added the Ministry of State for Social Development to her Consumer and Corporate Affairs portfolio and her Status of Women responsibilities.

GÉRALD GODIN, member of the Quebec National Assembly for the Parti Québécois in the riding of Mercier (Montreal), was born in Trois-Rivières, Quebec, in 1938. Educated at the Seminaire St. Joseph in Trois-Rivières, he pursued a career in journalism, first with *Le Nouvelliste* in Trois-Rivières, then with *Le Nouveau Journal* in Montreal; he subsequently became Managing Director of Québec–Presse and taught journalism at the Université de Montréal and the Université du Québec. In 1976 he was elected to the Quebec National Assembly for the Parti Québécois in the riding of Mercier (Montreal). He was appointed Minister of Immigration in 1980 and the following year became Minister of Cultural Communities and Immigration, assuming responsibility for application of the various aspects of the Charter of the French Language (Bill 101), except the chapter concerning the language of education. One of the founders of the review, *Parti pris,* he was director of the publishing house Parti pris from 1969 until 1977. A poet and short-story writer, he has published six volumes of poetry: *Chansons très naïves* (1960), *Poèmes et Cantons* (1962), *Nouveaux Poèmes* (1963), *Les Cantouques* (1967), *Libertés surveillées* (1975), and *Sarzenes* (1983).

VICTOR C. GOLDBLOOM, President and Chief Executive Officer, Canadian Council of Christians and Jews, was born in Montreal, Quebec, in 1923. He received his M.D. (1945) from McGill University, where he subsequently taught for many years. In 1966 he was elected to the Quebec National Assembly for the Liberal party in the new riding of D'Arcy McGee (Montreal). In 1970 he was appointed Quebec's first Minister of the Environment, becoming the first member of the Jewish community to be named to the Quebec Cabinet; in his six years in this portfolio he was responsible for Quebec's Environment Quality Act and the creation of the province's Environment Protection Services. In 1973 he was also named Minister of Municipal Affairs, and, in 1975, Minister Responsible for the Olympics Installation Board. He resigned from the National Assembly in 1979 to become President of the Canadian Council of Christians and Jews. Since 1982 he has also been President of the International Council of Christians and Jews. He received an honorary degree from the University of Toronto (1980).

ROBERT KROETSCH, University Professor, University of Manitoba, was born in Heisler, Alberta, in 1927. He received his B.A. (1948) from the University of Alberta, his M.A. (1956) from Middlebury College, and his Ph.D. (1961) from the University of Iowa. From 1961 until 1978 he was a member of the Department of English, State University of New York at Binghamton; in 1978 he became professor of English at the University of Manitoba. He has published six volumes of poetry: *The Ledger* (1973), *The Stone Hammer Poems* (1975), *Seed Catalogue* (1977), *The Sad Phoenician* (1979), *Field Notes* (1981), and *Advice to My Friends* (1985). He has also written seven novels, *But We Are Exiles* (1965), *The Words of My Roaring* (1966), *The Studhorse Man* (1969), *Gone Indian* (1973), *Badlands* (1975), *What the Crow Said* (1978), and *Alibi* (1983); a travel book, *Alberta* (1968); an autobiographical account, *The Crow Journals* (1980); a volume of literary reflections, *Labyrinths of Voice: Conversations with Robert Kroetsch* (1982); and several critical articles. He was one of the two founding editors of *Boundary 2: A Journal of Post-Modern Literature*.

H. IAN MACDONALD, Professor, Faculty of Administrative Studies, and Director, York International, York University, and Chairman, IDEA Corporation (Innovation Development for Employment Advancement), was born in Toronto, Ontario, in 1929. He received his B. Com. (1952) from the University of Toronto and his M.A. (1954) and B. Phil. (1955) from Oxford University. In 1955 he joined the Department of Political Economy, University of Toronto. In 1965 he was appointed Chief Economist for the government of Ontario, in 1967, Deputy Provincial Treasurer, in 1968, Deputy Treasurer and Deputy Minister of Economics, and in 1972, Deputy Minister of Economics and Intergovernmental Affairs. From 1974 until 1984 he was President of York University.

BOB RAE, leader of the Ontario New Democratic Party, was born in Ottawa, Ontario, in 1948. He received his B.A. (1969) and LL.B. (1977) from the University of Toronto and his B. Phil. (1971) from Oxford University. The author of articles on political theory, Canadian politics, labor law, and industrial relations, he was Special Lecturer in Industrial Relations at the University of Toronto (1976–77). In 1978 he was elected federal member of Parliament for the New Democratic Party in the riding of Broadview-Greenwood (Toronto) and served as the party's housing critic and later as the party's finance critic. He resigned his federal seat in March 1982 to become leader of the Ontario New Democratic Party. He became a member of the provincial Legislature in November 1982 when he won a by-election in the riding of York South (Toronto).

DAVID STAINES, Professor of English, University of Ottawa, was born in Toronto, Ontario, in 1946. He received his B.A. (1967) from the University of Toronto and his A.M. (1968) and Ph.D. (1973) from Harvard University. He has published many articles on medieval romance and drama and Arthurian literature, and the book-length study *Tennyson's Camelot: The Idylls of the King and Its Medieval Sources* (1982). In addition to his publications in the medieval field, he has written introductions to Sylvia Fraser's *Pandora* and Margaret Laurence's *The Diviners* for the New Canadian Library. He compiled and edited *The Canadian Imagination: Dimensions of a Literary Culture* (1977), *Responses and Evaluations: Essays on Canada by E. K. Brown* (1977), *Reappraisals: Morley Callaghan* (1981), and *Reappraisals: Stephen Leacock* (1986). In 1982–84, he took a leave of absence from the University of Ottawa to be Five College Professor of Canadian Studies and, in the second year, Director of the Five College Program in Canadian Studies.

WALTER STEWART, Professor and Director of the School of Journalism, University of King's College, Halifax, was born in Toronto, Ontario, in 1931. He attended the University of Toronto, but left before graduating in order to pursue a career in journalism. He worked for the *Toronto Telegram*, the *Toronto Star Weekly*, and *Maclean's;* for the last, he was Ottawa editor, Washington correspondent, and, later, managing editor. He has also been a frequent contributor and commentator for radio and television. Among his many books are *Shrug: Trudeau in Power* (1971), *Divide and Con: Canadian Politics in Action* (1973), *Hard to Swallow* (1974), *But Not in Canada* (1976), *As They See Us* (1976), *Strike!* (1977), *Paper Juggernaut* (1979), *Canadian Newspapers: The Inside Story* (1981), *Towers of Gold, Feet of Clay: The Canadian Banks* (1982), and *True Blue: The Loyalist Legend* (1985).

EP209x